Smarter Decision-Making

Organizational Management

The impact of decision-making in today's business environment is more critical than ever due to the acceleration of information and messaging.

As business leaders we constantly make decisions that impact our staff members, teams, companies, and organizations. Getting it right with respect to positive outcomes and effective decision-making is critical to our success at every level.

Given the rapid advancements in technology, our messages are spread over a global network in a matter of seconds leaving a permanent record that cannot be erased or taken back. Therefore, it is more important now than ever to avoid making poor decisions by listening in a way that is effective, deliberate, and responsible.

This book is the first in a series of Reality Based Leadership (RBL)© books written with the goal of sharing strategies and proven techniques for managers and leaders at all levels within any field of business.

The concepts, principles, and ideas shared are rooted in experience, and the knowledge gained serves as a foundation for success across a wide range of applications.

Smarter Decision-Making

Avoiding Poor Decisions through Effective Listening

Louis J. Pepe

ROWMAN & LITTLEFIELD
Lanham • Boulder • New York • London

Published by Rowman & Littlefield
A wholly owned subsidiary of The Rowman & Littlefield Publishing Group, Inc.
4501 Forbes Boulevard, Suite 200, Lanham, Maryland 20706
www.rowman.com

6 Tinworth Street, London SE11 5AL, United Kingdom

Copublished with Association of School Business Officials

Copyright © 2020 by Louis J. Pepe

British Library Cataloguing in Publication Information Available

Library of Congress Cataloging-in-Publication Data

Library of Congress Control Number: 2019949258
ISBN 978-1-4758-5454-1 (cloth : alk. paper)
ISBN 978-1-4758-5455-8 (pbk. : alk. paper)
ISBN 978-1-4758-5456-5 (Electronic)

This book is dedicated to the girl who believed in me from the start—my true love and lifelong best friend—Simona.

My inspiration is drawn from iconic leaders in history who came from humbling beginnings only to rise up and achieve great feats, Alexander Hamilton and Abraham Lincoln and influential authors, James C. Collins and Steven Covey along with contemporaries who continue to impart wisdom, knowledge and mentorship—special among them, David G. M. Clover, retired school business administrator, mentor, and United States Marine.

Contents

Foreword

By Jeffrey D. McCausland, PhD

Listening, not imitation, may be the highest form of flattery.
—Dr. Joyce Brothers

In this book Louis Pepe provides leaders in any walk of life an essential lesson—listening is perhaps one of the most important things any leader can do to ensure his or her success as well as the overall success of their organization. This seemingly simple, straightforward thought is fundamental, and has been for leaders throughout history. It underscores an essential point that leadership is now and has always been about the relationships between human beings.

It is critical, however, to understand that leadership and management are different, as we tend to use these terms interchangeably. Management focuses on work standards, resource allocation, and organizational design. How do we control complex institutions? While there is a Venn diagram for leadership and management, effective leadership is focused on developing trust, moving people as well as organizations into the future, and dealing with change. As President Dwight Eisenhower once said, "Leadership is the ability to decide what has to be done, and then get people to want to do it!" If any leader is going to get the maximum "buy-in" from his/her team to "want to do it," they are going to have to elicit the thoughts and ideas from throughout the organization. They are going to have to listen. Rear Admiral Grace Hopper was the first female naval officer promoted to the rank of admiral. She was often referred to as "Amazing Grace" and was a pioneer in the development of computer language. Grace often said throughout her career, "You manage things; you lead people."

But this lesson is not as simple as it may sound! As Louis suggests, "listening" is a skill that can be developed through careful thought and reflection. It is not simply our willingness to wait quietly for our next opportunity to speak! Furthermore, in the rapidly changing environment of the twenty-first century we are continually distracted by a barrage of information coming from cell phones, laptops, social media, and so forth, that can often get in the way of the essential need to listen and reflect. This also requires us to listen without "judgment." Acting immediately or responding to an impulse to solve a problem may not be always be appropriate and could actually be counterproductive. As a leader, remaining calm so that you can fully digest what you are being told is essential not only to avoid bad decisions but also to further develop the lines of communications within the organization.

Our understanding of effective listening must embrace the notion that communication in any organization is the exchange and flow of information, so it is often more than just words. Effective leaders realize that the context of any conversation and efforts to avoid ambiguity are crucial to keeping the organization focused. This means that leaders must be culturally aware, particularly in the modern age. They should consider body language—their own as well as others'. Finally, their actions must be consistent with their words.

Throughout the book Louis provides the reader with guidance, helpful tips, and a perspective—in essence, a road map for effective listening. Many if not all of these are key takeaways that any leader can implement almost immediately. They are clear, concise, and appropriate for a leader in any profession or sector of society. The case studies used, such as Merck and JetBlue, as well as the thoughts and ideas of leadership practitioners serve to make *Smarter Decision-Making* not only readable but enjoyable.

It is reported that President Abraham Lincoln, who was very well known as a storyteller, once said, "God gave us two ears and one mouth because he was trying to tell us something." Louis Pepe reminds leaders once again of the wisdom of those words and their value.

Preface

Keep your eyes on the stars and your feet on the ground.
—Theodore Roosevelt

Reality Based Leadership (RBL)© A conceptual framework of common sense!

Louis J. Pepe, CFO, MBA, RSBA

The RBL series is written based on my thirty years of management experience in building, managing, and leading teams to achieve desired outcomes while completing tasks, implementing strategies, and accomplishing goals. This is necessary in any organization to accomplish the ultimate objective—the mission.

Each book is meant to provide a glimpse into differing facets of organizational management that allows for continued success through refinement of skills promoting operational awareness in today's rapidly evolving world of business.

Avoiding poor decision-making is like ducking a punch to the face—no one wants a black eye. Yet that's exactly what a poor or even bad decision is for any company or organization; however, in many cases it too could be avoided by ducking or in this case listening.

The expression "like a fist on the eye" is meant to be something that goes together or fits like a glove.

I picked it up from my wife, who is German and never understood the relationship in the context she used it, as it seemed incongruent or the opposite of what was implied. When researching the meaning, I found it has evolved over time to be used as the opposite meaning to which is the context I have adopted for my title.

kavesinisukka:

English: It fits like a glove.
Spanish: It fits like a ring on the finger.
Italian: It fits like shoes painted on with a brush.

Finnish: It fits like *a . FiST. iN. the EYe . (ʃʼ ̈ʼ ʃʊ*

Not a subtle people, the Finns

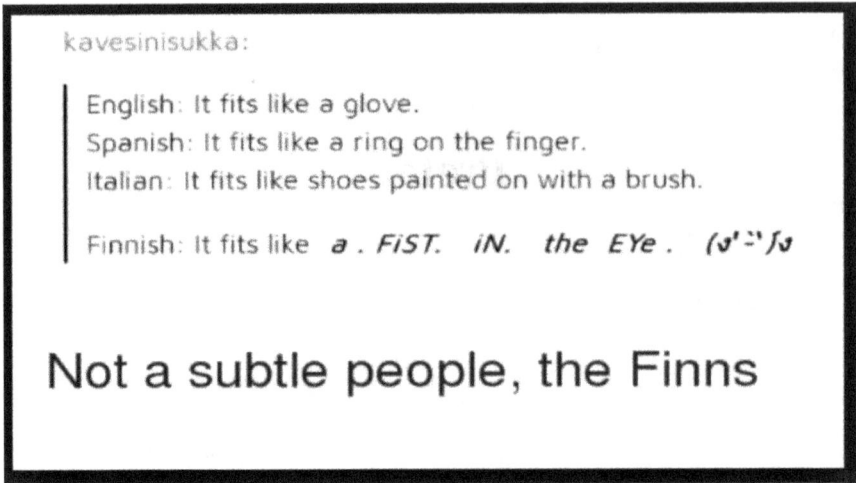

Figure 0.1. *Source: Reddit's blog post*

This expression and others coined by Martin Luther have permeated the German language. Sayings like "to move a mountain" and "pride comes before a fall" have even crept into English. Other more colorful ones are still used nowadays in German without a second thought, such as "fits like a fist on the eye" and "to bite the sour apple"—which in English has evolved into "bite the bullet." When it comes to expressing human characteristics, hardly anyone has managed to "hit the nail on the head" as well as Luther (although that wasn't one of his!).[1]

The subject matter in this book is not just advice for the reader, it is tried-and-true evidence of success and failure experienced by many who miss the point or act in a way that disrupts, embarrasses, or simply fails to accomplish the required task at hand.

Over a thirty-plus-year career in leadership, team building, and management, this is something that I have learned and continue to improve upon with patience and humility.

I have found that the smartest person in the room is often the one listening—not constantly talking. The art of active listening seems simple to master, yet one must first learn to hear without judgment, action, or the impulse to solve. When we put aside our subjective nature and clearly focus on the message, we begin to avoid poor decision-making that in some cases stand out like a "fist on the eye"!

—Louis J. Pepe, Lincoln Park, New Jersey, 2019

Acknowledgments

I have to start by thanking the best listener I have ever met, my wife, Simona. From reading early drafts to giving me advice on the ability to convey my message, her honesty and intelligent feedback are deeply valued. Thank you, honey.

A very special thanks to our bright, brilliant, beautiful, and accomplished daughters Jessica A. Sental and Megan S. Slamb, whom I continue to learn from and lean on for advice and practical application of my leadership ideas and actions.

I'm eternally grateful to my secretary and confidant Jeannine Dotten for her real-life, honest advice, guidance, and support in chasing my dream of putting my thoughts and comments into writing this book.

I'm forever indebted to Pat George for putting me in touch with Tom Koerner at Rowman & Littlefield Publishers, Inc., and Jeff McCausland for guiding me on the book proposal process. It is because of their efforts and encouragement that I have a legacy to pass on to my colleagues and leaders in the many fields of management.

Part I

The Power of Applied Listening

Chapter One

Focused Listening

Developing Listening Skills
That Strengthen Understanding

To apply any skill with success, we must first master that skill in order to effectively apply it if we have any chance of accomplishment. Listening skills are no exception. The basic components of effective listening revolve around speaking and understanding. Our speaking must be clear, direct, and concise in order to gain the appropriate understanding of our message, intent, and communication.

To gain proper understanding one must learn to truly hear the message. Hearing is not the same as listening. Have you ever heard a song on the radio and started to sing the lyrics only to find when you see the lyrics that they are not exactly what you've been belting out? Of course you're alone, right? This is normal and a good example of thinking you heard what was said, or perhaps the message is just blurry and you decide to fill in the blank because you consider what the meaning is or should be. We cannot be bothered with fact-checking at times, since let's face it—we're pretty smart and we continue to hear the same message with the same recognition. As a result, we continue until the day someone corrects us.

Getting a song wrong is one thing, but what about a task, project, or presentation? Depending on the size of your audience and the importance of the task, it could lead to devastating consequences that in some cases are unrecoverable.

Research shows that most people can recall only 25 percent of what they hear, and of that portion, they remember only about 20 percent of it accurately. In his work on understanding and retention of information, Edgar Dale, PhD, a former superintendent of schools in Webster, North Dakota, provided an intuitive model of the concreteness of various kinds of audiovisual media. This information has been debated based on accuracy; however, it demonstrates the concept that what we hear is not always what the message actually was or what was intended.

The closer we are to the message, experiential learning, or "hands-on," the more accurate our recall and therefore understanding of the meaning. This is true of any subject or message. We must therefore apply ourselves to deeper listening in order to overcome the odds of forgetting or simply thinking we have "the message" when we clearly do not.

Figure 1.1 represents the percentage of information retained when listening (20 percent) versus reading (10 percent).

Focused listening starts with hearing the person communicating with you by giving them your undivided attention. In the example above of the words to a song, most of us are doing something that requires our attention or focus, such as driving, working, or exercising, that pulls our attention from the active listening and therefore allows for gaps, misunderstanding, or in our case entirely different wording.

"All eyes on me." Ever hear a coach say this to a group of players either on the field or in the locker room? He is looking to ensure all members of the group are focused and listening to him without any distractions. He knows

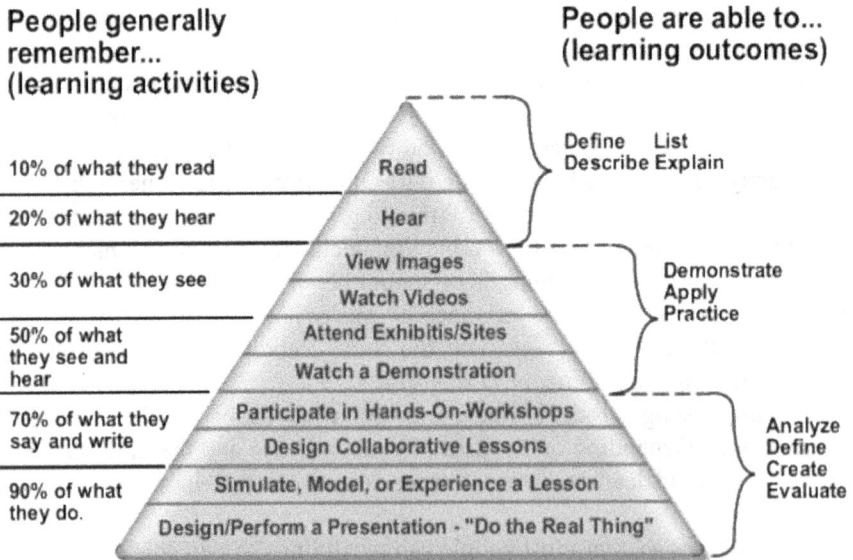

People generally remember... (learning activities)

People are able to... (learning outcomes)

Learning activity	
10% of what they read	Read
20% of what they hear	Hear
30% of what they see	View Images / Watch Videos
50% of what they see and hear	Attend Exhibitis/Sites / Watch a Demonstration
70% of what they say and write	Participate in Hands-On-Workshops / Design Collaborative Lessons
90% of what they do.	Simulate, Model, or Experience a Lesson / Design/Perform a Presentation - "Do the Real Thing"

Define List Describe Explain

Demonstrate Apply Practice

Analyze Define Create Evaluate

Figure 1.1.   Cone of Experience. *Source: https://en.wikipedia.org/wiki/Edgar_Dale*

this could mean the difference between poor execution or even a missed opportunity once the game is on.

When we give someone our eyes and ears, we catch inferences to their demeanor (gauging the intensity or importance of the subject matter) that may or may not be congruent to the tone or pitch of their voice. The eyes open the mind to process in tandem with the hearing of the message, resulting in better overall understanding. Likewise, it gives the communicator a sense of the listener's understanding. Ever explained something to someone who has that glazed or confused look when you finish? You immediately know that they don't get it. Now consider that they weren't looking at you when you spoke. Better yet, they give you the nod or grunt or simple "Yeah"—this is a false understanding that leads to getting it wrong.

It's the same for leaders in every profession. Consider a surgeon describing a difficult operation to the team she is going perform surgery with. An exact understanding of the surgery beforehand is essential to minimize the risks associated with that surgery. She cannot afford anything but clear understanding of the steps to be taken while the operation is in process and expects total adherence to commands given at crucial intervals throughout the surgery. Would you want any less of this team if you were the patient? Should we expect any less of our teams when the success of our department, group, or organization is in play? Especially when you are the one held accountable for the results.

Take for instance the outcome of the Civil War in America. Could a misunderstanding have changed the course of history and laid the groundwork for the State of the Union circa 1865? One such example is found to have made the Top 10 Times Miscommunication Had Awful Consequences:

The Battle of Antietam (also known as the Battle of Sharpsburg) is undoubtedly one of the most recognized battles in American history. It was fought on September 17, 1862, near Antietam Creek in Sharpsburg, Maryland. What most people don't know is that this iconic battle only happened due to a misunderstanding by the commander of General Robert E. Lee's rear guard, D. H. Hill. While leading his army in the North, Lee dispatched movement orders to a few of his generals. The orders detailed how he would maneuver while dividing his forces slightly. Due to a misunderstanding, the orders were accidentally left behind at a campsite. Not long after the troops moved on, a Union soldier found the orders and they were passed up to George McClellan, the Union's top commander. Knowing the Confederate army's plans, the Union army was able to move in and attack Lee in the Battle of Antietam. Not only did this misunderstanding result in over twenty-two thousand casualties in the bloodiest single day in the history of America, but it allowed Abraham Lincoln to issue the Emancipation Proclamation, freeing all slaves in the South.[1]

Let's be clear: Although generated out of a misunderstanding and paid for by a high cost of human life, the misunderstanding produced a pivotal victory for the North and led to one of the hallmark decisions of the Lincoln legacy—the emancipation of the slaves on September 22, 1862. As a result, the misunderstanding was devastating for the South and began to turn the tide for the Union.

So how do we improve or develop listening skills? As educators, we are constantly giving directions, explaining concepts, or demonstrating strategies to students that require active listening in order to attain a mastery of the concept(s) or learn the skills necessary for problem solving. Simultaneously we continue to improve our teachers through planned professional development opportunities to gain and improve the knowledge and skills important to their positions and job performance. In order to reach the desired outcome, the teachers must apply the same listening skills they teach their students or the process will fall short and any growth will be short of what was intended or possible. As facilitators of the learning, we hope that our students are listening carefully to our lessons and assignment instructions. As administrators, we hope the same is taking place with our professional staff as they participate in their growth opportunities. Unfortunately, distractions exist for adults as much as children, and we find that sometimes they aren't paying close attention to what is being said or they simply miss key information that later leads to failure or breakdowns in process or actions. The same is true in the professional world with personal devices such as cell phones. Next time you're in a learning environment with adults, look around the room and you'll be amazed how many people are checking email, texting, or surfing the web while the speaker is speaking. The larger the room, the easier it is for the offender to hide under the cloak of anonymity . . . not anymore—it has become socially acceptable to ignore or disrupt the speaker by ensuring you portray the call or action as immediate and life threatening. Instead, lay the ground rules such as turn off all cell phones and get the audience's attention by demanding it up front and keep it by ensuring you are on topic, precise, and clear about the subject matter. If you're unprepared or lack the knowledge or ability to convey the information, you will lose the room for sure.

FIVE PRINCIPLES TO DEVELOP
OR IMPROVE LISTENING SKILLS

1. Eyes Front—Look at the speaker.
2. Check the Message—When in doubt, speak out!
3. Cull the Message—Break it down into important and relevant points.
4. Adapt the Message—Relativeness breeds familiarity.

5. Model Good Listening Strategies—Good leaders act, but first they ask, then listen.

Eyes Front — Look at the speaker

This is without doubt the number-one step to improved understanding of what is spoken. As easy as it seems, most of us are guilty of violating this simple principle. Eye contact is a form of body language that is important during communication. When you maintain eye contact with the person speaking, it indicates that you are focused and giving your undivided attention. It demonstrates your desire to hear the message and the importance you place on the conversation, briefing, or presentation.

Any motivational speaker knows it is imperative to ensure they not only make eye contact with their audience but that they maintain it throughout the presentation, especially when key points or critical information is being given. According to Sims Wyeth, president of Sims Wyeth & Co.,[2] "If there is one simple thing you can do to enhance your impact as a presenter, persuade others to see things as you see them." This makes your audience more likely to accept your ideas. In order to maintain their attention, purposeful eye contact with one person at a time remains essential.

Eye contact is part of everyday communication, and an audience can feel dismissed or overlooked if they are denied it. Making eye contact with individuals brings them into the discussion and gives them a sense of involvement in your presentation. They now become willing participants in the experience rather than just people taking up seats. It personalizes the message and allows you to connect with your audience on a personal level that helps to convey your objectives. It keeps it real and relatable; you know when you have them, as they begin to talk with their eyes and their own body language that confirms you got their attention.

Check the Message — When in doubt, speak out!

You know the old saying—Don't assume, it makes an "ass out of you and me." Let's face it, if you're not sure about what was said, then it wasn't properly conveyed or it's complicated information that needs to be simplified. The sender of the message already knows the subject matter and what they expect in the form of desired outcomes or actions. Instead, check the message by asking the speaker to repeat certain parts or provide clarification. Better to admit a lack of understanding than proceed with something that you are not sure of or even worse, do the wrong thing based a real misunderstanding.

Ever complete a project or difficult assignment only to find it was not the one expected to be completed, and instead you wasted time and manpower?

Imagine working on a presentation that takes the better part of a weekend. Convinced you have nailed it, you wait for Monday morning to present it to your boss only to find that he or she meant for a different approach, and while they like the slides, it isn't what they wanted, and therefore the entire presentation has to be reworked. The point is, had you done a better job of listening to what they wanted to capture or probed deeper into what you heard during your initial planning meeting, you could have saved yourself work and gotten it right the first time.

This is a persistent challenge in advertising firms when attempting to launch a new campaign with a client. "Got a rocky relationship with a client? It probably comes down to communication. And to communicate better, you need to know what clients really want."[3]

In a 2017 report issued by Up to the Light, a leading provider of client surveys to the UK design industry, this fact was underscored through 455 client interviews commissioned by design agencies. On the topic of client development, 77 percent of clients believed that their design agency could provide more added-value communication.

Hence the need to do a better job of listening to what is sought or needed in attempting to capture the essence of a design, plan, or objective when meeting with your own groups. This is where probing allows you to flesh out the true desire and intent that avoids unnecessary trips back to the proverbial drawing board. This is how and why you need to "check the message."

Cull the Message—Break it down into important and relevant points

By zeroing in on the relevant or important aspects of the message, we are essentially thinning the "herd" or in this case making smaller the amount of information "heard." When presenting volumes of, or dense, information, it's better to break it up into smaller bites. Small, chewable chunks are easier to digest. When you are in the process of explaining a difficult or significant issue, put this advice into action. For example, let's look at something that concerns us all in any business—our cash position. If positive, anyone is happy to give the report, and more often than not, it is an easy conversation. On the contrary, a report on a negative cash position is paramount to waking up on the day of a scheduled root canal—not fun.

By culling the message or breaking it down to its basic components of *cause and effect* along with *degrees of impact* or *elements of change*, we start to frame the discussion in a way that bolsters the confidence of both the speaker/presenter and our audience. This is based on trust, competency, and credibility. CFOs deal with this when considering a downturn in sales or revenue, and government finance officers deal with this in addressing declines in or loss of tax ratables. Couple this with higher than expected expenditures due to unanticipated costs and you have a negative effect on cash available. The concept is simple and straight to the point and perhaps the best advice regarding presentation of material—right in line with the KISS principle (Keep It Simple Stupid).

Likewise, financial advisers do this when reporting a negative financial impact involving large figures. While the total figure is large, the breakdown gives a better understanding of how and why smaller numbers add up to the overall impact. Presenting the *cause and effect* in connection with a timeline allows boards of directors, shareholders, managers, or the public to grasp the complexities of the problem or see the various issues that contributed or led to the final outcome. Let's face it, it's easier to throw out a large number when it's positive; however, it too must be explained and at the same time allows for your message to demonstrate the intricate steps, processes, and procedures employed in the day-to-day management of that business. This aids both the revealer (speaker) and the listener (target audience) in promoting better understanding.

Adapt the Message

Relativeness breeds familiarity, hence better understanding of key elements or concepts. Adapt the message to specific events or tasks of familiarity. Messages are often geared to get concepts across that benefit the listeners by providing guidance or instruction to accomplish or improve situations. While no two situations are identical, they are many times parallels to the challenges organizations face. In specific situations that involve directives or regulations such as laws, policies, or procedures, the listener needs to know how the information pertains to them, their department, or their organization as a whole. In these cases, the information is geared to an expected adherence and must ensure clear understanding as it is required for compliance. The listener must be sure to comprehend the meaning and expectancy of the instruction. By aligning the message to your particular set of circumstances you begin that process. Once you can put it in the proper terms, you are able to concretize the message and ensure success in its application. Think along the lines of what you have done in the past with such information or similar situations and the mechanics of how you in turn applied it to a positive outcome.

Model Good Listening Strategies

How can anyone expect others to listen when they speak if they do not afford the same courtesy to those in their charge? Demonstrating that you are a good listener not only improves overall relationships, it signals what is expected and the importance that you as a leader place on this particular skill. Good listeners are good leaders. A good leader checks their ego at the door and allows for other thoughts to refine or even modify a decision. If we had all the answers or already knew the optimal actions needed to succeed, we would not require teams or colleagues, professional associations or conferences. Hence we would stop improving and never grow and develop as leaders. We learn from others and even learn from teaching.

Adjunct professors across the country experience such opportunity to learn from others in the various graduate courses they teach each year. The richness of the information and personal experiences give them a golden opportunity to improve their own skills by hearing how other professionals apply their knowledge, skills, and views on various issues they are confronted with in their own organizations. Without listening, the professor would continue to operate based on their own experiences and therefore fail to consider improvements or other options to problem solving.

As educators we are lifelong learners—this statement is predicated on the understanding that we are still acquiring knowledge and experience to add to our acumen. Ever looked at a problem for days or weeks and still come up with the same result? Although your methods may be sound and the outcome sufficient, a better solution could be out there and may only come to light upon further reflection and discussion with others. That is the very basis of collaboration and good decision-making. Problem-solving skills involve research, flexibility, and information sharing to arrive at optimal solutions.

The only way the exercise works is when people truly listen and give equal weight to the thoughts of others. Sometimes the solution is right in front of us like a "fist on the eye" or blatant. It is glaringly obvious, undisguised or unconcealed. Yet absent your ability to listen, you would have missed it and thus aided in poor decision-making that you, your team, or your organization will suffer for, and worse, you will be remembered by your subordinates as closed off and unsympathetic or indifferent to their contributions. The result—they will stop talking and, whether you know it or not, stop listening.

Case in point: a roof hatch. Facility inspections are often conducted prior to undertaking a facilities project to determine deficiencies present and prioritization of projects.

In one particular walk-through, the school business administrator, referred to in the industry as the BA, was explaining to the principal that the director of facilities and the district's architects had identified a major section of roof as a candidate for complete replacement. At the time they were joined by the building's head custodian. The BA introduced a new practice of involving custodial/maintenance personnel in all facility walk-throughs to ensure adequate input and discussion prior to final development of any bid specifications by the architects and/or engineers.

The purpose of this action is to get the "inside scoop" or "firsthand" information about the problems, issues, or ideas for improvements from the men and women that are tasked with daily maintenance and upkeep of the buildings. The goal is to avoid unnecessary change orders down the road once the project is in full construction, as change orders equate to cost over-runs that eat into contingency budgets (unforeseen or unanticipated modifications). Not only are you forced to add scope or additional contractor services, the costs are further increased by markup both by the architect and the contractor that can add anywhere from 10 to 15 percent on average.

The other point to consider is that once you go to bid, the scope and details of the project are set. Once awarded, there is no major deviation from what was specified, and therefore any ideas for major improvements beyond that scope are lost opportunities, as you only get one bite at the apple. Likewise, it's easier to reduce, cut, or trim the initial concept or scope of work than it is to retrofit or alter the project later. Projects delayed or postponed by a year or more can add even more as these projects see cost escalation in materials and labor at about 3 percent per year.

So on the walk-through the BA decided he wanted to go on the roof and get a firsthand look at what they were dealing with as well as an aerial view of the grounds from a better vantage point. The head custodian proceeded to walk down the hall and stopped in front of a window overlooking the roof on the second floor. He asked the group to give him a minute, and he returned with a milk crate. They looked questioningly at him as he put the milk crate in front of the radiator and opened the window, giving them detailed instruction on how to step onto the crate, then onto the radiator, bend down and place one leg through the window, and kind of shimmy out onto the roof. Forget that they were in suits; what about the potential workers' compensation claims that could arise out of injuries?

The BA looked at the head custodian and asked the obvious question—don't you have a roof hatch? The response was nothing short of disappointing, as he said, "No, we don't. I've been asking for one for years and nobody listened. Finally, I stopped asking." The district added a roof hatch to the plans before they were finalized and sent out to bid. Even more concerning was that they found they had the same situation at two of their other schools.

This district is no exception; many businesses or organizations run into this problem of "lack of listening" by those in charge regarding concerns or suggestions for improvements. "Nobody ever asked me" or "nobody ever listens to us" are statements made by staff members in similar situations who are closest to the issues and problems we are trying to address and solve.

Good leaders act, but first they ask, then listen. A new show came out on NBC recently called *New Amsterdam* about a hospital in New York City. What struck me most about the lead character, Dr. Max Goodwin, whose mantra is "break the rules—heal the system," is his continual question to everyone he comes in contact with under his supervision: "How can I help?" "What can we do better?" While it makes good TV, it makes better sense. If we aren't listening as supervisors, how can we improve operations and boost morale?

Never discount the power of an idea or suggestion based on where it comes from in the organization chart; a lot of times those at the bottom of the chart have the best ideas and commonsense approach that lead to the largest accomplishments. That's not only modeling good listening strategies, that's good business.

Chapter Two

Considering "Meaning"

The Purpose of Meaning and How to Get There

Meaning is the central focal point of any conversation of value. The ability to connect with a listener or group of listeners is the desired result of any speaker and is critical to avoidance of miscues or unwarranted actions that lead to unwanted or undesirable results. *Value in our conversation* is how we get there as a speaker, delivering the message in a way that is concise and valuable to the listener. In order for decision makers to avoid poor decisions, they must be able to grasp the meaning or nature of the direction, warning, instruction, or lesson.

Figure 2.1 demonstrates the communication process in messaging.

As a listener, we get there *by being receptive to the messages that come our way*, with a willingness to hear new ideas or consider other points of view. It starts by being approachable, accessible, and receptive. This ability opens the lines of communication for subordinates as they feel valued and trusted for their input, ideas, and thoughts. While this does not mean that every thought or idea will be acted upon, it does mean that you as a leader are willing to receive their message or suggestions prior to taking action.

Think about a radio and listeners in an area. The better the reception, the more channels you pick up and thus more influences on your daily thoughts. More channels mean more opportunities to become exposed to different genres and a myriad of advertisements and news items. These are all stimuli that, once received, trigger impulses from neurons in our brain that allow us to begin processing the various messages.

By selecting alternate stations, you are broadening the experience of the messages you hear and the thoughts that follow. By listening to a broader

Speaker (value) **Message** (meaning) **Listener** (receptive)

MEANINGFUL CONVERSATION

Figure 2.1. The Communication Process

group of opinions or thoughts, you walk away with a bigger picture or reservoir of information to draw from in making any decision regardless of how important or time sensitive. Sometimes this is done informally through "one-on-ones" or smaller group meetings, and sometimes this is done over longer time periods with established or appointed groups. This is why committees work so well on the big and difficult decisions that require input and thought from area leaders on various levels within and sometimes from outside the organization, depending on the impact of the decisions that need to be made.

This process strengthens decisions that eventually rest with you as the leader for the ultimate success of any plan.

Webster's defines *meaning*[1] as serving as both a noun and an adjective, but its first purpose as a noun is considered to be "the thing one intends to convey especially by language—Purport." The second case covers "the thing that is conveyed especially by language—Import." So in essence importing is the listening portion of the import/export of communication. As an adjective, the act of conveying or intending to convey meaning references the words *significant* and *meaningful*.

In education this serves as the heart of what we do as educators with the goal of providing meaningful instruction. Without this, listening is a waste of time, as the listener is not getting anything of value (purpose) and therefore the activity falls short of its aim (direction). The same is true in any conversation between individuals, groups, or organizations in any line of work. Regardless of the topic, meaning is the most important element of the discussion and the only way a listener can actively stay engaged.

Sometimes it's *not* what we say, but what we *don't* say that creates the problem or misunderstanding. Today the very word "misunderstanding" has become synonymous with "excuse" or a cover for unintended consequences. "I'm sorry for any misunderstanding," or "Well, it was obviously a misunderstanding!" The reality is the misunderstanding exists and we are left to deal with the fallout. Stronger accountability is the only deterrent to avoidance of this type, and strategies to improve overall communications are key to avoiding the confusion.

There are times when the listener hears the message and understands the meaning as it is clearly conveyed, yet they turn to the speaker and say, "What do you mean?" It's not that they misunderstood or even have a real question about the message—in this case the listener just refuses to accept the message and the question is a defiant act or rebuke. This serves as the basis for another type of discussion called an argument. It happens more than one would think or like to admit.

This type of behavior can prove damaging for the listener. Instead of taking the meaning for its value or intent, the listener rejects the merit or importance of the message only to set out down the wrong path that ultimately leads to failure. This was the case in my next story—"Cliff Notes."

I came across an administrator who mastered the art of listening to gather the highlights through "one-on-one" updates from area content managers, building-level administrators, and cabinet members. It was pure genius the way he kept abreast of major items and issues within or confronting the organization in order to converse with the board of directors, city officials, and support groups. His subordinates dubbed him "Cliff Notes."

Where he failed to connect, where he missed the mark was in the details. He couldn't explain or follow important elements of actions or activities because at some point in every conversation he stopped listening or simply distrusted the person speaking to him. It was jolting at times the way he ended a conversation so abruptly that you were dismissed before you got to the meat of the issue. Ultimately this led to one problem after another for the very groups he was responsible for.

One time a building principal and this administrator were standing in the lobby of the school and the administrator challenged the principal, wanting to know why security equipment had not arrived yet. The principal was taken aback and replied, "Because you said no when I wanted to order it the first time." The decision to process the order came only after others outside the district stated they did in fact need the equipment to enhance building safety. That was exactly what had been conveyed months earlier by his team.

This was also the case of a sergeant first class (SFC) at Fort Campbell, Kentucky. Assigned to the 101st Air Assault Base as part of the US Army's Information Systems Command (USAISC) in the mid-1980s, we were responsible for maintaining the base's military auxiliary radio station or (MARS). I led a two-man team assigned to manage and restore the station's operations.

AAR4USH (the station's call sign) had once been a vital player in the region, taking charge of the area network in order to direct message traffic during peak hours. The goal was to facilitate accomplishment of the MARS mission . . . "To provide Department of Defense sponsored contingency communications on a local, national, and international basis."[2]

The station had become all but nonexistent in the recent years leading up to this time. Monthly hours of on-air time had hit a low of under ten hours and had lost the distinction of running the Kentucky-area net.

Six months later we had reentered various regional networks, erected new high-frequency antennae, and increased the monthly participation time well over 150 hours per month and had once again become a relevant station in the area, receiving recognition from the president of the Kentucky Association of Amateur Radio Operators.

The communication process was facilitated throughout the southern region, encompassing states that included Alabama, Florida, Georgia, Kentucky, Mississippi, North Carolina, South Carolina, and Tennessee. We had reassumed the Kentucky Area Net management responsibilities for amateur radio operators at two different times per day and conducted phone patches with Korea and other overseas stations in order to pass messages for soldiers to their families.

Word of our success had even caught the attention of a general out of Fort Gordon, Georgia, who scheduled a site visit.

The SFC decided to take an immediate interest in the station and the three-man squad to prepare for the general's visit. On the day of the general's arrival he was front and center to give the guided tour of our radio station and take credit for the accomplishments that led to the visit.

After the third question from the general and the SFC's third delay before turning to me for the explanation, the general stepped between us and began to converse directly with me on the finer points and details of the station and how we increased the operational efficiency. The general commended the team for our actions, pointing out how it strengthened our ability to accomplish our mission. He knew. Like the other example above: the SFC's misstep was in failing to get the details through a lack of interest and poor listening in briefings over the prior months.

In each case the individuals demonstrated a shortcoming based on their inability to listen and accept information from subordinates. In both cases this weakness presented them in a poor light and proves out the quote, "Leaders who don't listen will eventually be surrounded by people who have nothing to say" (Andy Stanley). They failed to act because they failed to listen.

Applied listening is taking meaning and putting it into action. Many times listening requires action or doing what you're told. This begins with trust, credibility, and authority. Listening to the wrong people can lead to doing the wrong thing. When we put our trust or faith in those who have our best interest at heart, whether it be for personal advancement and success as in the form of a mentor or a leader looking to move the company forward, we all win. When we disregard smart advice or clear direction, we in turn suffer as individuals or as a group.

The purpose of meaning is to provide direction, guidance, and assistance in completing activities and actions that either improve, safeguard, or prepare us for what lies ahead in life, our work, and personal growth. To succeed in any of these areas requires a strong understanding of the role and importance listening skills play in our daily lives. When you do something with purpose, you do it with determination. When your activities have purpose, you have a clear concept of what is important and you go after it with intent and motivation. Absent this, you simply flounder and produce results that are either short of the goal or mediocre. In some cases, they result in poor decisions that harm you and others.

How often have we heard the phrase "The meaning of life" as perhaps the biggest question we are all trying to understand in order to master the ultimate challenge . . . finding peace and purpose for our lives. The answer to this ever-present question revolves around the significance of existing in harmony within our own universe. Without meaning we lack purpose, without purpose we simply drift. Let's face it, it's a big ask that no one truly has the market cornered on with respect to the appropriate or correct response. However, to aid us on this journey, we have been supplied with idioms designed to convey meaning in all sorts of situations with figurative implication that differs from the literal meaning in an effort to provide better understanding.

These idioms are helpful and a smart way for many leaders to reach wide audiences, as they are based in simple logic and serve as a tool to allow the listener to grasp or arrive at the meaning quickly. The point is they work. Some idioms have become commonplace in today's organizations, such as:

- Bite the bullet

    Meaning: To get an unfavorable situation or task accomplished since it needs to get done.

- Caught between a rock and a hard place

    Meaning: Making a choice between two unpleasant or difficult choices.

- Crunching the numbers

    Meaning: Spending considerable analysis on reviewing financial impacts.

- Having skin in the game

    Meaning: You are personally invested in the outcome or process.

- The elephant or 800-pound gorilla in the room

    Meaning: An issue, person, or problem that someone is trying to avoid; and

- Think outside the box

    Meaning: Coming up with a creative solution to solve a problem in a way that produces a better outcome.

Meaning allows individuals to understand expectations both up and down the chain of command. Leaders utilize messaging to accomplish tasks and reach goals through the attainment of objectives. Carrying out directives requires a firm grasp of the subject matter, which is the intent or expectation in all instruction. In order to achieve proper conveyance of those instructions, we need to follow seven basic principles of understanding.

SEVEN PRINCIPLES OF UNDERSTANDING

1. Messages need to be clear, concise, and accurate.
2. Understanding is facilitated through clarity of purpose, intent, and instruction.
3. Understanding requires a mastery of the concept(s) sought, expected, or taught.
4. Know your people and their capabilities. The practices and activities in which they engage shape what is learned and how to employ it.
5. Experiential learning provides knowledge and familiarity. Individuals use what they already know to process and construct new understandings.
6. Messages need to be understood and not simply inferred. Test the reception.
7. Ensure that proper outcomes are reached by monitoring their progress and reviewing the process applied.

These fundamental norms encapsulate the rules of messaging needed to employ understanding.

While speed plays a vital role in the delivery of the message, proper understanding is everything. Without the understanding, the message is ineffective. While understanding remains paramount, much effort has gone into reducing the time delay between the sender and the receiver.

The time it takes to deliver a message has gone down considerably thanks to instant messaging; at the same time the number of messages we send has grown exponentially—hence the ease with which we message. Advances in technology and the ease with which we can message demand greater responsibility with regard to content. In the course of sending any message, our goal is to deliver that message with intent and proper understanding; so how do we get to the point of understanding in the quickest way? For starters—be specific!

Imagine you are commanding troops engaged in a battle and a message comes in saying "Take the hill" right before the radio cuts out and the reception is lost. OK, which hill? The one on the left? The one on the right? Or the one to your front? Without specific grid coordinates to aid in accomplishing your mission and avoid unnecessary casualties, you could be going after the wrong objective.

Now consider you receive a text from your boss and he says the project is a go. OK, again, which project? The one you're working on? The one you're contemplating? Or one of the three in the hopper? Again specificity rules out unnecessary attempts that waste time, energy, and manpower. Furthermore, it ensures that the message is received in the manner in which it was intended. Instructions are often sent with technology, and based on the quality, upkeep, and serviceability of both equipment and infrastructure there may be delays that could last hours or even days. Even cell phones are no good without signal service or power. Imagine sending the wrong message or sending a message that is unclear, and then your phone dies.

The Pony Express relied mostly on Morgans and thoroughbreds for their speed and stamina; however, once they reach their max, they too give out and need to recharge. Think back to all the westerns you've seen where the corporal comes riding into camp. The first thing he asks as he leaps off the horse with orders in hand is "Where is the commanding officer?" It is understood that *the message* he carries is highly important and time is of the essence in delivering that message to the appropriate person, in this case the commander. Notice those orders come at lightning speed, as the horse and courier are out of breath and covered in dust, signifying the urgency of delivering the message. Now consider the harmful effects if those orders (the message) are unclear or indistinguishable.

Without applying these principles, the message will be lost or go unheeded, as back in those days another rider with a fresh horse would need to be dispatched to go and get clarification or a new message. This was not only impractical, but the time delay could prove fatal, as in the opening story of the Civil War reference.

Time has always served as a hurdle to overcome in messaging that has given rise to improvements, beginning with smoke signals. Carrier pigeons date back to as early as 1150 in Baghdad and were also later used by Genghis Khan. They were an important part of military messaging and stayed on the active list up until World War II. The nineteenth century saw major gains in shorting the time and space in which messages were sent and received. The electric telegraph was a major breakthrough dating back to 1837 as it introduced immediacy in messaging. It eliminated another once-vital connection of messaging, the Pony Express. Both the East and West Coasts were finally linked up by the transcontinental telegraph line. On October 24, 1861, the Pony Express was discontinued.[3]

Advances in technology have revolutionized the way we communicate. Introduction of the telephone in the late 1800s circa 1876 was by far the most significant technological breakthrough, becoming a major lifeline of businesses and creating instant two-way communications. Other one-way communication devices also served a prominent role, such as business machines like the fax machines in the 1960s and pagers. But no invention cleared the way for instant communications around the world from any location like the cell phone, first introduced by Motorola in 1974 only to take about twenty years to flourish in today's life as a necessity.

While we have conquered speed of message through instant messaging, email, and scanning, we are still bound by the seven principles of understanding in order to safeguard the importance of these messages.

As the mediums have made messaging quicker and easier, we need to be more vigilant than ever in applying the fundamentals of good communication in the messages we send. Speed often comes at the cost of accuracy. By not following these principles, we risk the harmful consequences of bad messaging or statements we make that cannot be taken back as they go viral with the same speed. In business this can be not only harmful, it can become a serious public relations (PR) nightmare.

Texting has been the most popular way to communicate for years, and 89 percent of consumers recently said they want to text with businesses (typically for sales, service, and appointments).

A blog appearing on textrequests.com states that American adults send and receive 32 texts per day, totaling 18 billion texts every day, 541 billion texts every month, and 6.5 trillion texts every year.[4] The breakdown shows with no surprise that the majority are coming from eighteen- to thirty-four-year-olds or the millennials, who average around 101 messages per day sent and received. They have clearly mastered the technology they have grown up with as compared to the fifty-five-plus group or baby boomers, who accounted for an average of 16 text messages per day sent and received.

The rise and popularity of messaging apps have made this even easier, breaking down barriers such as cost as they are transmitted via Wi-Fi versus SMS (short messaging system) or cellular signals.

One popular app, WhatsApp, allows a sister on the East Coast of the United States to send her brothers text messages in Germany and receive responses in real time; they just need to factor in the six-hour time difference. Like most applications they start through personal use, but quickly turn into business applications once their familiarity and translatable use is discovered. "According to Pew Research Center, messaging apps boast high engagement rates and are popular among young consumers. Furthermore, in Nielsen's Facebook Messaging Survey, the majority of mobile messaging app users explained that they are more likely to spend at a business they can message directly."[5] "Like the original version of WhatsApp, the business application allows you to interact with customers in the form of a chat. However, unlike the normal chat, small business owners are offered a number of tools to help organize, automate, and speed up the communication process."[6]

President and cofounder of BusySeed Deutschland UG, Jenblat warns of the obvious challenges to instant messaging for business, starting with availability and security. Remember, these apps are device to device and therefore one-on-one along with limited security and unlimited exposure. They are, however, evolving and finding their place with small business. According to a recent post on Nerdwallet.com, "Business apps increase productivity and can make the life of a small-business owner easier."[7] The post features the 25 Best Small-Business Apps in 2019.

Regardless of intent, messages are only as good as they are interpreted by the receiver. If misunderstood, they are weak and ineffective. Avoiding poor decisions means they must be interpreted with the same meaning as they were written. This requires true understanding from the receiver . . . the individuals responsible for making our organizations run.

Demonstration of understanding is different from modeling in that individuals are able to show they understand what is expected by the work they produce. Therefore, they are acting in the way we expect based on the messages we produce. Leaders who model behaviors that are expected in their people demonstrate how they should behave, perform, or act. This difference is key to measuring the progress toward the goals we are responsible for. A lack of understanding or loss of meaning exhibits a clear concern regarding proper or anticipated actions and thus requires immediate intervention to reassert the intent.

Chapter Three

Considering Context and Avoiding Ambiguity

Context is what frames our discussion and provides the listener with the essence or meat of the conversation. It is what drives the message and delivers the clarity of purpose for the discussion. Without it we simply expend words and create ambiguity that hinders the listener from achieving the results or actions we seek.

So how do we avoid it? We can start by ensuring we first understand the message we wish to convey to the listener or group before us.

Ever been to a workshop or presentation and you walk away with no idea about the message or relevance? It leaves you wondering if you've just made a hard left and entered the "twilight zone." Perhaps they themselves are clueless about the subject matter or in some cases just poor speakers.

As students, we are taught to look for context clues that help us frame the subject matter to better understand the lesson or story. This is no different when trying to grasp the point or message of a high-level presentation or follow detailed instructions to navigate tasks assigned in response to an individual or team project.

Sometimes it depends on the culture or practices of the speaker. Therefore, how does the context of culture contribute to understanding the meaning? In today's global environment cultural context is more important than ever. A great example of this is provided by Barbara Adams, organizational psychologist, to the question "What is the meaning of 'cultural context'" (March 22, 2016). She explains that in the United States, when someone asks for your business card, it is appropriate to just hand it to them in a casual manner. The person asking knows that the contact information is on the card, and it would seem inappropriately self-important to make a big deal of the request or call attention to the card. In contrast she refers to the same action in China. She states, "It is expected that I will, with both hands, formally present my card to the person making the request. And it is expected that I will receive their card with the same formality. The card is seen as an extension of the person, and should be treated respectfully." Missing this important insight into Asian culture could have irreparable damage on the new relationship you are looking to foster and result in the loss of a sale.

Cultural context becomes more evident as individuals travel abroad for the first time on business or vacation. Europe, for instance, has many small countries, allowing one to travel easily from one region to another like the United States. However, territorial differences in language and other cultural aspects make them unique and place a high degree of importance on the need for understanding what is important and what is not when conducting business.

Social context involves understanding the makeup or character of individuals to know how they respond to certain social cues. Where they come from and how they think is based on generations of experiences, likes, and dislikes along with values they hold as a people that make up their culture. "A crucial facet of the social context is the status relationships have amongst various people. As a result of this actuality the social context means that people usually change the way they communicate in accordance to the proclaimed status of the person whom they are engaging with."[1] Ignoring this fact can leave your messages off the mark or even worse, a form of insult.

The importance of cultural savvy was reported on in an article that appeared in *Forbes* stating, "Intercultural savvy is vitally important—not just because they have to deal increasingly with globalization, but also because the work force within their own national borders is growing more and more diverse."[2] Understanding the culture is key to unlocking the region for business relationships.

Let's face it, we communicate all day every day in so many ways, both big and small. Every time we engage someone in communication we are messaging, and whether we realize it or not, we expect that those we speak to are on the same level regarding our meaning and the context in which we disclose our thoughts. While it seems obvious, it is not always true. Think about the importance of globalization with respect to the makeup of various nationalities in your own organizations. Globalization of the workplace means many of the cultural cues we would apply to trips out of the country are now needed within our organizations.

By missing context clues we can inadvertently isolate the receiver by either expecting they understand the message or utilizing words and gestures that alter their perception, interpretation, or simply are off-putting. "I have no idea what you mean" or "I don't know why he reacted like that"—sometimes these thoughts occur when you're working and communicating with people from different countries.[3]

This challenge continues to grow as more than one million persons obtained lawful permanent residence in the United States in 2017 alone, according to immigration statistics provided by US Homeland Security.[4] The changes we see are well beyond a region or continent, as immigrants today are coming from more than two hundred countries encompassing five continents.[5]

Certain thoughts and actions that are second nature to us as Americans are seen as rude or disrespectful to those in other cultures. Likewise, many times we have seen visitors from other parts of the world in America, and we think their behavior or mannerisms are not appropriate for our culture.

What we are doing is considering the "social" context by considering our immediate surroundings and code of behavior for business or personal engagement. The larger "cultural" context is all-inclusive, taking into consideration the broader global society in which the action occurs. As Adams explains, "It incorporates learned values and shared attitudes among groups of people. It includes language, norms, customs, ideas, beliefs and meanings. This is why, before travelling to a foreign country, it is helpful to learn about the culture of a country and its people, so that your behaviors can be placed in context while visiting."[6] Bottom line, it's a small, small world—after all!

Ambiguity is the enemy of clarity. It leaves the door open for doubt, uncertainty, or more than one interpretation of what is what. The lyrics of a popular song by the English punk rock band The Clash[7] lays it out there in simple terms: "Should I stay or should I go?" Should we proceed or should we stop?—that's the real question. These are basic questions that members of your staff, team, department, or group need to know, and they need to be sure they are proceeding in the correct manner and heading down the right path. Are they still on track to reach the desired destination or have they missed a turn or taken a left when they should have gone right or simply proceeded to truck on down the road? In order for listening to be correctly applied, one must understand the message with precision or the group will be out of sync. Smaller conversations during the process can serve as confirmation that the group is in fact on the right road or more importantly get them back on track if they are not. This provides confidence and shortens the trip, resulting in gains in efficiency and better outcomes, saving time and money.

Imagine a guide on a treacherous trip shrugging his shoulders in responding to a major decision, such as which path to take in navigating a river crossing or climbing a mountain. You look to the guide as your leader and have the confidence that he/she will see you through the perils of the trip in as safe a manner as possible to keep the adventure from becoming a disaster. That's what they do . . . and that's what we expect of them.

Robert Edwin Hall[8] was a New Zealand mountaineer best known for being the head guide of a 1996 Mount Everest expedition that ended his life. Hall died, along with a fellow guide and two clients. The tragic incident became a movie in 2015—*Everest*,[9] detailing the fateful trip up the mountain in their attempt to reach the summit. Although tragic due to the unforeseen weather conditions that overtook the expedition, Hall was the epitome of a leader who gave clear direction and direct guidance, which recognized him as New Zealand's intrepid mountaineer. Ambiguity or uncertainty in instructions had nothing to do with the tragedy, just the opposite. Had it not been for his clear direction, focus, and experience, the entire team would have perished. What got him there was his reputation for delivering the goods. In 1992 he started guiding amateur climbers on Mount Everest. With his company named Adventure Consultants, he successfully led nineteen clients to the summit without a single fatality.

The same is true of leaders in our organizations. They should serve as guides to ensure that we properly navigate the various challenges we face every day at our jobs. That's what they should do . . . and that's what we expect of them. When leaders fail to do this, they not only fail themselves, they fail us. This same understanding and link to leadership can be found in Christopher Maxwell's book *Lead like a Guide*,[10] in which he compares the approach of mountain guides to business and personal success while introducing six leadership strengths of world-class mountain guides: demonstrating social intelligence; adopting a flexible leadership style; empowering others; facilitating the development of trust; managing risk in an environment of uncertainty; and seeing the big picture. All these strengths found in these guides are demonstrated through active listening and imparting clear direction. In their world, ambiguity has no place. In their world, people listen or they die.

Context provides perspective. When it comes to safety and security, you need to listen like your life depends on it; your job just might, or the lives of others. Sounds a bit dramatic, yet how many times do people miss clues from those in crisis that could have avoided a large-scale incident involving fatalities or injuries? In today's world, workplace violence and school shootings have become an unfortunate part of our lives with an increase in both frequency and severity.

Let's look at avoiding poor decisions through effective listening in the context of casualty avoidance related to school shootings and workplace violence. Can effective listening aid in circumvention of these tragedies?

Every year, two million American workers report having been victims of workplace violence.[11] In 2014, 409 people were fatally injured in work-related attacks, according to the US Bureau of Labor Statistics. That's about 16 percent of the 4,821 workplace deaths that year. In 2018 school shootings have risen to a record number, as 113 people have been killed or injured in the United States.[12] According to Vox Media, Inc., an American digital media company based in Washington, DC, and New York City, "2018 was by far the worst year on record for gun violence in schools." In a December

10 article by German Lopez, the group reported data showing there were more incidents and more deaths in 2018 than any other year on record going back to 1970.

Parkland, Florida, lit up the news sites across the nation as a troubled youth, Nikolas Cruz, a nineteen-year-old former student, returned to Marjory Stoneman Douglas High School with a rifle and opened fire on students and staff after pulling a fire alarm. By the time the shooting stopped, seventeen people were killed, and seventeen others were injured. But why had Cruz done this awful thing in the first place? What led a former student to return to his school and open fire on random victims? Leading up to the shooting, Cruz had gone through a series of tragedies in his own life that led to violent and inappropriate behaviors culminating in his expulsion.

According to student disciplinary records obtained by the *Sun Sentinel*, Cruz had disciplinary issues going back to middle school, where he had received detention and suspension for multiple instances of foul language, insulting people, disobeying teachers, and disrupting classes. [13] In January 2017, Cruz assaulted someone and received a one-day internal suspension. The school asked for a "threat assessment" on him, the records indicate.

Figure 3.1 illustrates the number of school shootings across the United States in 2018 resulting in at least one death.

During the interrogation following the shooting, Cruz told Broward Sheriff's Office detectives that he had been hearing a voice or demons speaking to him for years—right up until that morning and the night before. [14] He claimed it started after his dad died when he was little and that it had gotten worse since his mom died in November, three months before the shooting. He described it as the voice of a young man, about his age, speaking inside his head. The question remains—was anyone listening? Did he reach out for help or leave contextual clues that foreshadowed the tragic event? Could effective listening have prevented this?

He said the only person he had ever told about it was his brother, referring to the voices. At one point, he asked to see a psychologist and said he had never seen one before, though other records indicate he had received mental health counseling and treatment in the past. Cruz said he tried to kill himself at least twice in the months and years before the massacre. On the first occasion, he said he was lonely and binged on vodka, tequila, and wine.

Depressed after his mother's death, he said he attempted suicide again two months before the shooting. He said he took a large dose of over-the-counter drugs, including ibuprofen and Advil. He survived both attempts, he said.

Cruz said he had gotten in trouble, but hadn't been prosecuted, for shooting at a chicken with his pellet gun when he was about thirteen.

Three chilling cell-phone video recordings Cruz made, outlining his deadly plans before the shooting, were made public by the prosecution in May.

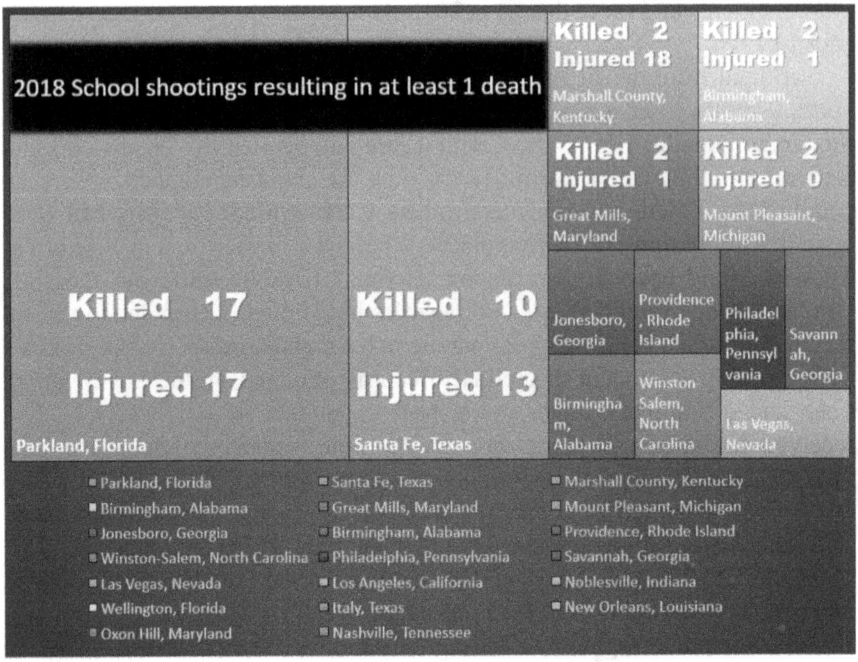

		Killed 2	Killed 2
2018 School shootings resulting in at least 1 death		Injured 18	Injured 1
		Marshall County, Kentucky	Birmingham, Alabama
		Killed 2	Killed 2
		Injured 1	Injured 0
		Great Mills, Maryland	Mount Pleasant, Michigan

Killed 17 | **Killed 10** — Jonesboro, Georgia / Providence, Rhode Island / Philadelphia, Pennsylvania / Savannah, Georgia

Injured 17 | **Injured 13** — Birmingham, Alabama / Winston-Salem, North Carolina / Las Vegas, Nevada

Parkland, Florida | Santa Fe, Texas

- Parkland, Florida
- Birmingham, Alabama
- Jonesboro, Georgia
- Winston-Salem, North Carolina
- Las Vegas, Nevada
- Wellington, Florida
- Oxon Hill, Maryland
- Santa Fe, Texas
- Great Mills, Maryland
- Birmingham, Alabama
- Philadelphia, Pennsylvania
- Los Angeles, California
- Italy, Texas
- Nashville, Tennessee
- Marshall County, Kentucky
- Mount Pleasant, Michigan
- Providence, Rhode Island
- Savannah, Georgia
- Noblesville, Indiana
- New Orleans, Louisiana

Figure 3.1. Number of School Shootings across the United States in 2018 with One or More Deaths. *Source: https://en.wikipedia.org/wiki/List_of_school_ shootings_in_the_United_States*

Cruz was a ticking time bomb that had encountered local law enforcement, health professionals, trained psychologists, school guidance counselors, teachers, administrators, fellow students, and family members, yet no one saw this coming? Had they all missed the context clues when he was speaking? While it is easy to speculate and point fingers after any tragedy, the reality is we need to do a better job of listening to those in distress. Now you understand the context of my statement—you need to listen like your life depends on it.

USA Today reported that as recently as January 2018, one month before the shooting, the FBI received a tip about Cruz and his "desire to kill people," but the information was never forwarded for investigation, the bureau later confirmed.[15] The article goes on to report that in a written statement, the FBI said a person close to Cruz contacted the agency's tip line on January 5 to report concerns about "Cruz's gun ownership, desire to kill people, erratic behavior, and disturbing social media posts, as well as the potential of him conducting a school shooting." The informant was not identified in the FBI's statement. "Under established protocols, the information provided by the caller should have been assessed as a potential threat to life," the FBI said.

The US Department of Homeland Security launched an active call-to-action campaign designed to engage all citizens in the effort to protect lives by reporting suspicious activity: "If you see something, say something"; that's good, clear direction with meaning, but let's expand it to include listening: "If you hear something, do something."

Without context the sayings are unusable and ambiguous. Say something about what? Hear something about what? They demonstrate the need for context in order to avoid ambiguity and allow the listener to take the appropriate steps in the call to action. That is putting active listening to work. Together these actions combine to increase our efforts for casualty avoidance.

Part II

The Importance of Meaning

Chapter Four

Ready, Set, Listen

Why Most People Today Can Not Wait to Talk

The listening process declines significantly when an individual is more interested in getting their own thoughts or comments out there in front of those who are already speaking. In these situations, they are more focused on what they are about to say and are not averse to interrupting or verbally hijacking the conversation to get there. What they want is to dominate the conversation, or so it seems to the individual who has the floor and those around them.

This situation is further challenged by the generational differences that exist in organizations, and depending on the setting, it can intensify the negative feelings that ensue from the person being interrupted. With more generations than ever working together at the same time, we are in the midst of a new workplace phenomenon consisting of as many as five generations:

* Traditionalists—born before 1946
* Baby boomers—born between 1946 and 1964
* Generation X—born between 1965 and 1976
* Generation Y, or millennials—born between 1977 and 1997
* Generation Z—born after 1997

Like cohorts each generation has common experiences that normed them and similar viewpoints, preferences, and values. They have a much easier time listening to each other, as they have similar understandings of the material and context of their discussions. Put two boomers in the room and they start talking about vested interests such as career goals, market issues, and family in a structured and disciplined way. They are the generation that like rules, order, and plans and expect loyal efforts on the part of their employees.

Put two Generation Zs in the room and they will be heads down, texting or swiping the screens on their devices. As digital natives, their lives revolve around handheld devices that are as comfortable to them as a watch would be for a traditionalist. In order to have our messages received effectively, we must ensure that we are on the right frequency with all groups.

While generational issues represent differences in groups, they do not account for the interruptive behavior of those who stop listening only to talk. According to therapist Alan Piper, co-owner of Wise Blue Owl Therapy Centre outside of London, UK, it starts with selfishness and controlling factors: "There are many reasons, one of the main ones is that people that interrupt before someone else has finished generally want to say something that is on their mind concerning the subject being talked about. (Their opinion is more important, or so they believe.) Often they are not listing to what the other person is saying."[1]

Beyond generations, there is also the difference in sex. Women are frequently interrupted by men, and according to the *Harvard Business Review*, female Supreme Court justices are interrupted more by male justices and advocates.[2] "From the kindergarten classroom to the corporate boardroom, men and women are socialized to communicate differently." In an article written by Leslie Shore, "The most problematic issue that arises from this discrepancy is the disproportionate number of times that men interrupt women."[3]

Why does this matter? Because every time managers allow this to happen, they are settling for less than the best as they forgo input that could prove essential in making better or correct decisions that result in better outcomes. The reality is women are advancing and assuming leadership roles in higher numbers at more organizations than ever in modern history.

"Since the 1990s, a growing body of research has sought to quantify the relationship between women's representation in leadership positions and organizational financial performance."[4] Their input is essential to good decision-making and avoidance of poor ones. In an article titled "The Business Case for Women Leaders: Meta-Analysis, Research Critique, and Path Forward," Jenny M. Hoobler, Courtney R. Masterson, Stella M. Nkomo, and Eric J. Michel produced the following statement of evidence: "Commonly known as the 'business case' for women's leadership, the idea is that having more women leaders is good for business. Through meta-analysis ($k = 78$, $n = 117,639$ organizations) of the direct effects of women's representation in leadership (as CEOs, on top management teams, and on boards of directors) on financial performance, and tests that proxy theoretical arguments for moderated relationships, we call attention to equivocal findings."[5]

Women in these leadership positions offer great thought, energy, and direction for any organization at any level. As such, they deserve to be listened to without interruption and encouraged to speak out, comment, and deliberate with the same value and weight as men.

Hoobler, Masterson, Nkomo, and Michel's research results suggest women's leadership positively affects the firm's performance and increases sales. In fact, they prove it benefits women's leadership—overall and, specifically, the presence of a female CEO—is more likely to positively relate to firms' financial performance in more gender-egalitarian cultures. [6]

Nobody wants to get interrupted; however, it happens, and the reality is it will continue if left unchecked. As leaders we need to ensure the benefit of all discussion to avoid missing potential counsel, better ideas, or optimal solutions in problem solving. Likewise, these voices if left extinguished or halted could be providing warning or bringing underlying issues to the surface that need our attention.

Another theory behind the interruptions is one of conversational styles and the way individuals engage in communications with others.

Katherine Hilton, a doctoral candidate in linguistics at Stanford, reports that American English speakers have different conversational styles. Her research has identified two distinct groups: high- and low-intensity speakers.

- *High-intensity speakers* are generally uncomfortable with moments of silence in conversation and consider talking at the same time a sign of engagement.
- *Low-intensity speakers* find simultaneous chatter to be rude and prefer that people speak one at a time in conversation.

This lends itself to the fact that sometimes it's just a race to get to the finish line or deliver the goods in the conversation, the point. Individuals inherently want to get a jump on the competition, be the first across the line, the first to answer the question or break the news, especially when it's positive or seen as an opportunity to demonstrate smarts, initiative, or overall prowess. This is heightened during any meeting involving large groups of colleagues that consists of peers. While they are all colleagues in their given profession, they are not all peers. Peers consist of individuals within an organization or service sector and even industry that are on the same level within those organizations, aka "the competition." Overt or not, they are all vying for the same recognition and ability to display their personal "value add" in the form of expertise, effectiveness, mastery, talent, or genius. This group can include supervisors, administrators, directors, and even cabinet-level officers.

The real challenge is to sit and wait for the opportune moment to raise your hand or interject your view, fact, or opinion on the topic "du jour," hoping that it resonates with the leader(s) of the group as well as everyone in the room. This is how good teams utilize collegiality to promote effective behaviors, honest discussion, and information sharing or brainstorming that benefits the group as well as the individual. That should be and is the goal of any effective organization, group, or team that leads to positive and consistent results.

The opposite is to jump in and blurt out a thought that leaves you wishing you had remained a listener instead of a speaker who obviously failed to achieve your objective or just plain got it wrong. The gaffe or impulsive response is only exacerbated or underscored when you make a feeble attempt to restate that view, fact, or opinion in a manner as to avoid embarrassment, criticism, or snickering while you sink a little lower in your chair and start looking at your notes, waiting for the moment to pass. Although inappropriate and even harmful to a positive exchange of ideas, the allowance of others to mock a speaker is evidence of a poorly run meeting. Even though it happens at times, it should not. In the absence of good leadership, it is allowed to stand.

A good leader, however, takes control of the meeting and does not permit others to get a laugh at the speaker's expense. In this instance the leader or facilitator of the meeting has an opportunity to listen and gauge the interactions from the individuals in the room and then act in a positive way by effectively admonishing the inappropriate behavior or negative actions of those in the group (not necessary the individuals), thus supporting the speaker by encouraging or recognizing some element that is helpful or simply thanking them for their input but suggesting they consider an alternative viewpoint.

Distressing as it may be, it is a reality that befalls each of us at one point or another in our career, especially in the early stages, and as stated in the onset of this book, it is my attempt to share Reality Based Leadership (RBL)© points with the reader designed to avoid such blunders.

One person that comes to mind in such an example is a friend and colleague from Ohio, Jim Rowan. Jim is currently the executive director of the Ohio Association of School Business Officials and someone I have gotten to know over the years through ASBO International.

As a state officer in NJASBO, I attended various leadership forums across the country. One such program was the Eagle Institute presented by ASBO International and sponsored by AXA Equitable Life Insurance Company. The leadership institute is designed to promote the free exchange of ideas, thoughts, and practices of today's leaders that are aligned with leadership concepts from an academic, historical, and philosophical perspective.

On my last trip, the group led by Jeff McCausland, founder and CEO of Diamond6 Leadership and Strategy, LLC, had a dinner at the historic City Tavern Restaurant in the Old City section of Philadelphia. Jeff, a retired colonel from the US Army and former dean of academics at the US Army War College, was leading a discussion with the group reflecting on what we had learned throughout the day and how we could apply those lessons in our own organizations. The day was rich with subject matter and speakers on topics ranging from "Organizational Culture and Change"[7] to "Turning Negative Heat into Positive Energy."[8]

What followed was a quicker-than-needed volunteer in the form of a young man from the Ohio delegation eager to responded to a challenge question, which in turn he swung and missed completely. It was apparent he did not understand the context of the question, nor did he have a firm grasp of the subject matter. The immediate silence was evidence of this fact, and you could hear the undertone of chuckles that followed along with either eye rolling or visible discomfort in the other attendees. Jeff in turn responded as any experienced leader should and offered an engaging comment that displayed depth of thought while saying something to the effect of, "OK, that's interesting but not exactly what I was looking for." He thanked him for his input and began to seek other thoughts on the topic.

Now I don't exactly remember the comment, but I do remember the awkward feeling in the room and empathy that others and I felt for him at that moment. What I do remember, what I will never forget, is what was said immediately following the exchange. Jim stood up and addressed the group by stating that this young man had only recently been put into his leadership position in his district less than a year ago, and this was his first such conference. He went on to explain the sacrifice and commitment made by this individual to join us and that he expected great things from him in the future.

Wow! In two sentences he demonstrated his own grasp of what happened by listening to not just his answer but the reactions of the room. Not only did he defend his colleague, he supported him. He reinforced good leadership expectations when having a discussion and the importance of building individuals by demonstrating support. That's the power of applied listening at its core.

So how do we avoid situations like this before they become toxic? By establishing or setting ground rules in advance.

"When words are both true and kind, they can change the world" (Buddha).

Back to competition. The story of Jim and the open exchange of ideas on leadership in this type of venue provides opportunity for recognition and future opportunity to lead within the larger organization, in this case ASBO International. So again, we find ourselves in a situation involving colleagues and mostly peers (state officers from across the country) that form a group from which International candidates will emerge. Friendly and cordial as it may be, competition is afoot. I have found competition breeds success in higher attainment of goals and objectives. A challenge inevitably ups our game, refines our focus, and allows us to stand out in a crowd of peers. It should not evoke a cutthroat mentality but a healthy motivation to do better, to raise the bar and challenge our peers to bring their A game to every situation we encounter.

Competition is not always bad, and most people who dislike it are those who feel they can never win or outperform others. While teams work in tandem to gain extraordinary results, certain members of those teams are stars while others are solid producers or supporters. Look at any professional sporting team, baseball, basketball, football, hockey, or soccer. If you think competition is just between teams, you're either naïve or just don't watch sports. Although a successful team represents the virtues of comradery, togetherness, and personal sacrifice for the greater good of the team resulting in winning, its players are in constant competition with each other and themselves from the time training camp starts until the end of the season to acquire or maintain that coveted starting position or playing time on the field, court, or in the arena. That means someone is going to sit the bench or go inactive. This is not only healthy competition but good coaching as long as they remain on a level playing field with open competition and the rules are known and carried out fairly.

In our world that same realization means someone is going to get promoted or receive a larger raise or get the recognition that others in the same group, our peers, will not. I'm sure it has happened to you either way. Trust me, it is not always an easy thing to deal with, even when you are the one receiving the reward or getting the recognition. So how does listening help us achieve our goal of personal advancement in our field or company? By listening for that moment that makes sense and allows your contribution to effectuate the desired result. I would like to share four simple principles (PPSA) that will help you avoid this common mistake and allow you to succeed in these settings:

1. Prepare for Meetings—Preparation is key to understanding the message.
2. Pick your moment—do not rush it . . . wait for it.
3. Speak when ready—Don't let someone else grab your idea . . . go for it.
4. Accept the judgment—Feedback shapes our ultimate decisions.

Prepare for meetings

Preparation is key to understanding the message for any meeting. That's why agendas are critical to productivity in those meetings. One look at an agenda can provide an overview of what items will be discussed or acted upon and allows the attendees to prepare ahead of time for that discussion. If you're not sure about an item or the context of the discussion, remember to apply the strategy of *when in doubt, speak out.*

Follow up with a quick email or phone call to the individual responsible for placing the item on the agenda. More often than not, the degree of importance regarding selection of topics for discussion has been prediscussed informally such as through advice or sounding boards, or formally in an agenda-setting meeting. Clarity is desired on both ends of the discussion to allow that discussion to have value. Most individuals welcome the request for information (RFI). Plus, it shows the individual you are paying attention and care about making the meeting productive. Preparation by those involved will not only allow for rich dialogue and professional opinion, guidance, and consideration of viewpoints, it fosters an environment where fact-based or data-driven decisions move the organization in the right direction.

Being prepared demonstrates your willingness to lead, whether it be a discussion group, team activity, or project initiative. When speaking to my team members, I stress the point that you do not need to be in a leadership position to lead. Instead I promote the concept of leadership at every level. When we join or lead the conversation and prove to possess the knowledge and understanding of the problem, issue, or challenge, we reveal our strengths along with a mastery of the concept. A reciprocal nod of acknowledgment or definitive words of agreement give us an immediate confidence. Bingo! Assurance is one tool a leader has that provides immediate validation in the efforts of those under their charge. That praise and recognition can motivate and lead to further hard work and determination to "shine" again when called upon. Do not just show up—that's lazy, ineffective, and a waste of everyone's time. A lack of engagement or prolonged silence through multiple meetings leaves others wondering what you bring, if anything, to the team.

Pick Your Moment

Pick your moment—do not rush it . . . wait for it like a pitch. In order for a discussion to have meaning it must have thought. Try writing out your thought prior to interjecting it into conversation in a meeting. I do this sometimes while listening to others speaking, as it allows for conscious thought and gives me an opportunity to prescreen what I am about to say. Seeing the sense of it or having the ability to fine-tune it prior to putting it into the conversation provides for a more weighted contribution. Occasionally, I will draft an entire outline with key points and relevant ideas but wait for the right moment in the flow of the discussion to present the one(s) that are appropriate for that moment. In other words, I do not attempt to hold the floor for all my points at once, since this is not a presentation but a conversation. Accordingly, when I do speak, it is met with greater attention and focus, as the point is relevant to the matter at hand. Likewise, there are times when I simply sit back and listen to others who more closely hit the mark or cover the same ground, and therefore my comments are not needed.

Some people can monopolize the limited time we have for a meeting through continuous talking that simply fills the room with air; hence the phrase "long-winded." Notice the word choice "talking" versus "speaking" or better yet "conversing." A conversation evokes the elements of listening, thinking, and responding that constitute an exchange or back-and-forth. Constant talking is simply a one-dimensional rant that lacks the elements of a conversation. As such, it differs from speaking in that speaking provides information to the listener and therefore serves a purpose. Think about the people in your life who never find an end or leave you exhausted when listening to their talking. Odds are, if you are anything like the majority of people, you simply stop listening at some point and tune out. Kind of like my dad when we were in the car on a family drive. That man could drive for miles with my mother talking, the radio playing, and three boys chattering, bickering, pushing, and fighting in the backseat of his 1963 Dodge Dart and not listen to a word. He was in the "zone" and we were all "out"; hence the phrase "zoned out." That car later gave its life in 1975 climbing Pikes Peak in Colorado.

Speak When Ready

Don't let someone else grab your idea . . . go for it. In baseball, wait too long and the pitch will go right by you—strike! Delay enough and you strike out, left at the plate in dismay as you lost your opportunity to swing or take a chance at connecting and hitting the ball with the opportunity to score a run. It is the same in any meeting when you know the material, understand the meaning of "the pitch" of the discussion, and are ready to offer some good comment you have crafted and yet you hesitate. At that moment you lean in and start to talk, but someone else beats you to the punch, and their voice is the one that delivers the words you had at the ready. But now the ownership of the idea is credited to them. In a way, you have struck out and may not get another opportunity, as the meeting may be coming to an end just like the inning or even the game. This is a common problem with individuals who exhibit a pensive personality. This doesn't mean that others are smarter or better prepared, as oftentimes they are saying the exact thought or some version of what you have already concluded; however, in the competitive aspect of the group or team, they simply do not lack the courage or confidence to put themselves out there and risk the potential of being wrong.

In order to bolster assurance of success in being listened to or, better yet, heard, I evoke the modes of persuasion coined by Aristotle: ethos, pathos, and logos. They rely on ethics, emotion, and logic. Let's take a look at the basic definition, meaning, and usefulness of each approach:

Ethos *(sometimes called an appeal to ethics), then, is used as a means of convincing an audience via the authority or credibility of the persuader, be it a notable or experienced figure in the field or even a popular celebrity.*

Pathos *(appeal to emotion) is a way of convincing an audience of an argument by creating an emotional response to an impassioned plea or a convincing story.*

Logos *(appeal to logic) is a way of persuading an audience with reason, using facts and figures.*

This provides a basic framework to frame the discussion of your ideas or appeal in a way that is thoughtful, supported, and ordered. It essentially delivers the message with authority and reasoning. This is always a better way to proceed than just jumping in, to grab the floor and then begin to formulate a response with a lot of filler words to stall the discussion as you attempt to process your idea.

Worse yet is when you share your idea with a colleague going into the meeting only to see them put it out there as their idea and you are left with your mouth open in dismay as those in the room are congratulating the person for your idea. *Back to wait for it.*

This is clearly different from prediscussion of an idea with colleagues prior to the meeting to gain support or influence for the discussion that will take place on the issue in the meeting.

Accept the Judgment

Feedback shapes our ultimate decisions. Respect the views of others when discussing points, concerns, or issues. We know what we think and in most cases believe we are right or at least are prepared to make our point. Often the discussion is simply a way to gain approval and acceptance of the action or plan you wish to enact. Occasionally we are even looking for validation of actions we have already taken that have been met with controversy or pushback.

We must prepare for the answer that comes, as it is not always the one we seek. Although difficult to accept at times, we do better when we reflect on the thoughts and statements of others when they are not in line with our own. While it is easy to receive praise in the form of positive feedback, we improve and grow when we listen to the evaluative statements from others that point out weaknesses or deficiencies in our actions, thoughts, or procedures. Reflection requires listening. Absent reflection, we are not open to improvement, modification, or even changing course by abandoning our bad ideas. When people start giving your ideas nicknames, it's time to abort.

Consider the following story, "The Ferry Approach."

A particular school district was confronted with a major parking issue at one of their elementary schools that had reached an untenable point. There was an ongoing safety concern at this elementary school site regarding student drop-off and pickup. Each afternoon vehicles were observed double and triple parked on the street adjacent to the building. It was extremely dangerous, as students routinely ran in-between vehicles that were parked or in motion to reach their vehicle for pickup. Like many schools built in the 1930s, 1940s, and 1950s, the parking lot was not sized or configured to accommodate the volume of traffic and number of vehicles that arrived on site on a daily basis. Even though the students that attended the school were all considered "walkers," as with most community elementary schools they are mostly driven, as parents today are not keen on allowing their children to walk to school for a number of reasons starting with safety concerns. Bad-weather days only compounded the problems by adding additional elements of slick road surfaces. A new traffic plan was needed that allowed parents to queue up for student drop-off and pickup in a safe and efficient manner.

A committee was formed and a charge was written to develop a viable option to improve the circulation and traffic flow aimed at increasing the amount of faculty and visitor parking spaces by redesigning and expanding the existing parking lot. Working through a collaborative process of community stakeholders and public safety, city, and school officials, the group returned a recommendation to the superintendent of schools to redesign and enlarge the existing parking lot through site work that included pushing into the existing slope of the property by erecting a large retaining wall and relocating sidewalks and utilities. The price tag for the project was upward of $400,000.

Rather than accepting the recommendation, the superintendent advanced his own plan in which he believed they could accommodate approximately three hundred vehicles at one time on the asphalt playing area behind the school. The plan was to bring the cars through a single-lane access gate on a street parallel to the school and begin forming ten lines that would hold approximately thirty cars in a queue until all students were loaded and ready to be released. Upon release, the vehicles would flow into and through the existing parking lot to exit onto the main street.

His reasoning was based on a similar concept that had worked in another district he had been assigned to in the past. His "logos" or his logic was flawed for a number of reasons; chiefly, the two schools were different in many ways, starting with available space. The idea and plan was fraught with challenges and doubts, as it created new issues of concern including strict adherence, manpower, time delay, vehicle proximity, and the fact that the first car in would in fact be in the last row to exit, thus creating a wait time of anywhere from twenty to forty minutes. As cars entered the site, they would be queued in the lines and "frozen" until they were "released"; hence the "ferry approach." Add to this that all students must be in the vehicles prior to any cars exiting and that students and parents would need to connect prior to making their way to the vehicles. Remember too that we are talking about elementary students ranging from six to eleven years old. Parents were not happy to say the least and failed to endorse the plan. The superintendent called the plan "Freeze and Release"—the parents named it "The Stack and Pack in the Back"!

Failing to listen, and intent on proving its viability, he ordered a "pilot" of the approach, and they went through a week-long attempt to demonstrate its success. So what happened? Many parents chose not to participate and began finding alternative streets around the school to park in defiance of the plan. Neighbors complained about the excess parking on streets that never experienced this in the past. Parents who did participate started arriving later each day as they realized the pattern of "FILO" (first in, last out). A citizen-based committee organized within the neighborhood, led by parents and neighbors intent on eliminating the plan and providing alternative options.

The end of the plan came at the monthly school board meeting that was held in the school to discuss the plan's success and implementation. It was standing room only, it was ugly, and it failed miserably. The board was unanimous in recommending they go back to the drawing board and work with this group to find a better solution.

Six months later the district worked with the group to find an acceptable solution that addressed all needs. This led to the revival of the original plan presented by the architects and the original committee. A year later, the project was launched. It has been working flawlessly ever since.

The takeaway: accept the feedback and improve your plans.

Chapter Five

Credible Conversations That Matter

Say What You Mean and Do What You Say

Credibility is at the heart of trust and confidence. It answers the leadership questions of why: (1) Why are you in charge? and (2) Why should we follow you? Absent credibility, these questions are difficult or impossible to answer. In order for your conversations to matter, you must possess the credibility that carries weight and meaning once spoken.

If an officer of the law cites you for speeding, you must believe he has not only the authority but the credibility to uphold the ticket in court prior to deciding to challenge the second, as you know he possesses the first. So what gives him authority? It starts with the uniform, the badge, the patch, and of course the gun that gives them the credibility. It starts with how they handle themselves in the dispatch of their duties, the training they have completed, and certifications and rank they possess.

Lacking these fundamental elements, their credibility begins to diminish quickly, say for instance an unmarked car versus a decaled cruiser. Without the lights and siren, the unmarked car would not represent a credible threat and the officer would have a difficult time in pulling other vehicles over. What if the officer was out of uniform and they left their badge at home? There would be serious doubt as to any credibility, not to mention authority.

The uniform, the badge, the patch, the decals are all symbols of recognition. These symbols give them instant credibility; however, as they carry out their duties and interact with individuals, that credibility can wane or even dissipate if their actions are not in line with the very laws they are sworn to uphold.

It is no different in our world as managers, supervisors, directors, vice presidents, executives, or board members. Symbols such as title, size of office, business attire, diplomas, and credentials provide the instant credibility needed to begin answering the why questions associated with leadership that your people are thinking about even if they are not speaking out.

Symbols represent authority. They allow us to assume that authority similar to the officers discussed above; however, once we begin to interact with those in our charge and those we report to, we must "walk the talk."[1]

So where do we begin? We start by considering one hard fact—regardless of where you are in the organization's structure, as a leader your word must be solid, truthful, and direct. It is your bond, and as such must be honored and safeguarded. You must not allow others to compromise your own integrity or act in any way that is contrary to what you say or mean in grooming and supporting your own team. Basically your word is what you put out as an advertisement of fact, expectation, or promise. Whether in a one-on-one situation, group meeting, or public venue, that credibility is critical, and if breached could be fatal to the organization as well as you. Reputations are years in the making and vulnerable to broken promises, breached agreements, and compromised beliefs. When this happens, others can see it as a betrayal of their trust and confidence and in some cases are left wondering what you stand for once you've gone back on your word.

Like any situation, common sense puts the matter in perspective as to the degree of importance that resides with the issue. Likewise, we are not talking about changes in position based on new or relevant information that you come across in exercising your responsibilities to that person, the team, or a larger audience. How you handle the matter can likewise avoid the break in trust by letting the affected parties know in advance if possible as to why the change in course. When this is not possible, you should provide a feedback mechanism to explain the shift, thus ensuring better understanding for those affected. This is often completed through public relations channels, spokespersons, or formal memoranda; however, the personal conversation as an administrator or executive serves to lessen the blow and disappointment and restore the trust.

Concern is a compelling attribute and one that shares its place with sincerity. People respond better to the truth even if it's not good news than avoidance or untruth, especially when the bad news or untruth becomes spin. Just because outsiders may be mollified or soothed by a glossed-over version of the truth, those closest to the message (insiders) will not and as such become distrusting and suspicious going forward. The result is they will stop listening and worse yet stop sharing anything of value as they begin to mistrust you and the organization.

In a large break of trust the consequences are huge and, depending on the action taken, can end up with jail time. Look at Enron. The Enron scandal, publicized in October 2001, eventually led to the bankruptcy of the Enron Corporation, an American energy company based in Houston, Texas, and the de facto dissolution of Arthur Andersen, which was one of the five largest audit and accountancy partnerships in the world. In addition to being the largest bankruptcy reorganization in American history at that time, Enron was cited as the biggest audit failure.[2] This was so large of a trust issue that "Enron" became a metaphor for deceit, cover-up, and distrust with respect to any questioning of financial reports.

Case in point—three years after the incident went public, a school auditor was presenting the board of education with the annual audit in which there were no findings, a great thing if you're the CFO. A disgruntled individual in the audience, unhappy with the board's position on the collective bargaining agreement (teacher's association contract), stood up as asked the auditor, "So you're telling me that you looked at everything and did not find a single issue or finding?" The response from the auditor: "That is correct, we did not issue any material findings." His response, which he yelled out in an angry voice was, "That's what they said at Enron!"

The outburst went to the heart of that administration's credibility and questioned their trust with the board and public. In truth it turned out to be an attack on the board of education, who were in the process of negotiations with the teacher's union. The disgruntled member of the public was the husband of the union president.

The point is, the impact of Enron carried far beyond the corporation, and who if anybody wanted to hire Kenneth Lay, Andrew Fastow, or Jeffrey Skilling after that or after they got out of prison? Although this is an extreme case on a major scale involving illegal activity, the trust that was broken can have the same effect as in a small to midsize company where one of the principals is found to have concealed vital information or broken the law. Now consider you were a middle manager or among their staff at the time of the scandal. That's a tough position to be in and one that translates into severe mistrust. Unfortunately, in most cases individuals on your team are held accountable for your actions and are judged in accordance with your reputation. Think your word matters? So do your actions.

Clarity and honesty are two characteristics that Abraham Lincoln espoused regularly and held to be self-evident in carrying out the responsibilities of leadership for the country. As I spoke of in the dedication, Lincoln has served as hero to me for many reasons, most of all for his honest, straightforward approach to do and say what he believed to be right, fair, and in the best interest of mankind. Although we are not met with the tough challenges Lincoln faced upon his first inauguration, a divided nation on the verge of civil war, we are faced with different challenges and issues that leave us with sleepless nights, physical discomfort, and worry from time to time. But as with Lincoln, saying what we mean lays the foundation for doing what we say—the follow-through. It is what turns words into action and allows others to believe in our passion, our commitment, our promises. It also provides comfort in knowing we are steady and worth following. Even if they disagree with a decision we've made, they respect the fact that we are consistent and fair in our approach to decision-making. This can range from conflict resolution to reassignment of tasks or evaluation of personnel to name a few.

Donald T. Phillips wrote a whole chapter addressing this quality in Lincoln titled "Exercise a Strong Hand—Be Decisive" in his book *Lincoln on Leadership.*[3] In order to decide what he believed to be true and good, Lincoln consulted his cabinet members, political leaders, community leaders, and others, thus demonstrating his ability to listen. While Lincoln's decisions were not popular with many, they were understood by all. He had the ability to make the tough decisions and act swiftly once he was convinced they were in the best interest of the majority or country. This was further demonstrated in Doris Kearns Goodwin's book *Team of Rivals*[4] that speaks to the political genius of Lincoln in assembling opponents to staff and cabinet and then going on to convert them into supporters that became a steering committee who operationalized his ideas into actions taken throughout the Civil War. That's a quality we need in leadership positions. That's a quality people respect in their leaders. That is what allows you to be heard and others to listen in order to make better decisions because of it.

We each have people in our lives who exhibit this quality, and when you find them, more often than not they are successful, highly respected, and capable of earning our trust. They become trusted advisers in different aspects of our lives and we value them.

Three such people come to mind: an accountant, a real-estate agent, and a financial consultant. Each of these professionals exhibits traits that are central to positions of trust, such as detail oriented, organized, a mind for business, and an appreciation for capital gains. First and foremost, these individuals must possess a high degree of ethics and integrity. Notice the "high degree" attached to ethics versus integrity. There is a critical difference, as some professionals hold themselves to a higher standard where ethics are involved, as do clients; however, integrity is purely a have or have not. Who wants to work with someone who claims to have 90 percent or even 99 percent integrity? It's either 100 percent or nothing. It comes down to the relationship, results, and feel that builds and maintains trust with these individuals as we share our personal assets, planning, and future goals.

Effective listening is at the center of these successful relationships, and it begins with the professional exhibiting the same characteristics in effective listening that are seen in great leaders. These individuals need to evoke and apply listening to manage, advise, process actions, and make recommendations for future goals. Ultimately they must be successful in handling our needs. Trust is gained as we see measurable results that are clearly benchmarked against comparisons in each field, such as yield on investments, attainment of savings, or increased value in real-estate holdings.

Top sellers, top performers, and highly recognized individuals in their fields have one thing in common—they are often top listeners. This leads to recognition as top producers both in sales and performance, thus netting awards and recognition with the companies and organizations they serve, including the small-business community.

Boost Awards, a UK company pioneering the award entry consultancy market, understands the importance of validation and recognition of individuals and companies. They claim to be the world's first and largest award entry consultancy. This validates the importance placed on winning awards and attaining recognition as a top performer in your class to gain and maintain market presence and market share. The group provides a searchable list of awards by industry and by country or region, including the most credible American business awards from across all industry sectors, including US Finance Awards, American Marketing Awards, Silicon Valley Tech Awards, and many American Advertising Awards.[5] With more than three hundred awards in twenty-four industries ranging from Business to Travel and Tourism, it is clear that businesses value top performers, and that starts with active listeners.

That's why Business.com lists "Good Communication" as the number-one trait in 7 Qualities of Top Performers, citing, "Good communication is the ability not only to relay a message effectively, but to be an active listener. Top performers will be able to listen to their teammates effectively, provide clear feedback and instructions, and promote open communication within your office. Some signs of a good communicator are maintaining eye contact, asking questions, not interrupting and showing empathy for others."[6]

Top performers operate at a higher level of effectiveness than their peers for many reasons; however, for one they listen better. They have a good ear for what the client wants and what their needs truly are. Sometimes it means convincing the client that what they need is not necessarily what they want. Getting them to that understanding requires trust, confidence, and articulation of a vision or plan that resonates with them and offers a favorable outcome.

Successful accountants are masterful communicators comfortable with both verbal and written communication. Listening allows them to focus on client concerns, pinpoint areas of concern, and deliver findings and recommendations to improve internal controls and strengthen financial oversight of the organization and its financial reporting. According to the National Register on Vocational Education and Training (VET) in Australia, "Good accountants are ethical, diplomatic and have well-developed people skills that enable them to develop trust and rapport with their clients. They're able to use their integrity to foster collaborative and respectful environments, which helps clients make good business decisions."[7]

Good realtors have the ability to understand the needs of their clients and match those needs with the availability of the market. Putting buyers and sellers together requires tenets of effective listening, strong networking, and persistence in making it actionable through applied listening by matching the needs and wants with available inventory. Failure to listen to the client in this industry results in countless showings that waste everyone's time. At the same time, disregarding the advice of the realtor or mortgage professional by pushing beyond your purchasing limit will only end in disappointment and lost time when the loan application falls through.

Prosperous financial advisers like the accountants are adept at organization, financial analysis, and tax laws; however, this is where the difference begins. While accountants focus on tax implications, financial advisers are focused on income growth through investment and savings strategies. The common thread again is listening. Only through open and honest listening can the professionals we depend upon gain our trust and allow for the successful relationships to become lasting ones. Regardless of the returns, if a client has little to no appetite for risk, the relationship becomes one of distrust, stress, and hard feelings when there is a dip in the market or the stock goes down. Conversely, a client who has a high tolerance for risk expects to see large upswings in a bull market. The key to success for the wealth manager is to listen to the client and deliver in accordance with the acceptable risk limit for that individual.

The best of these individuals go beyond the work expected and take a personal interest in our own success. When we succeed, they succeed. When we fail, they fail. That is the type of commitment and caring that goes beyond good business—it becomes personal.

There are leaders among us in every profession who exhibit the same qualities of listening, caring, and taking action to benefit the lives of others. They serve to encourage and inspire us to do more and achieve our dreams that without them we could miss out on the opportunities that make us successful. In your own experiences you will find these types of individuals to be leaders who meant what they said and went beyond themselves to effectuate positive change in others.

Think about who on your team has done that and what characteristics they exhibit that you can incorporate into your own leadership style. That is modeling at its best. The takeaway is simple: what brings them all together from government to various industries and different companies is their ability to listen, process what they hear, and advise accordingly. In the case of the president, a nation listened and the Union was preserved. In the case of the accountant, realtor, and financial adviser, individuals listened and avoided poor decisions that would have had a material impact in their personal lives.

Chapter Six

Considering Language Structure

Oral Language, Syntax,
and Sentence Complexity

Reading is a form of listening. It provides the listener with detail, allowing information or instruction for higher-level processing to occur by avoiding gaps or loss of focus. These gaps or loss of focus happen when individuals are distracted and only hear or process bits and pieces of the message. When the message is large, written material avoids this gap if constructed well. Language structure is essential in conveying the appropriate meaning, and syntax and sentence complexity are dictated by the subject matter being considered. Syntax is defined as the arrangement of words and phrases to create well-formed sentences. In literature that placement is crucial to provide the reader with the appropriate meaning and the path to get the reader to the predetermined destination. The bigger challenge, and why this is so important, is that the reader or "listener" is not in front of you, so you lose your ability to read their body language, or clarify information as they digest it.

It allows a writer to provide explicit meaning in what they wish to convey. Writing has advantages over speaking, as it is lasting and allows the listener to reread and interpret the same message and process it at their own pace. The written information remains constant, as it has not been altered, as opposed to conversation that can change each time the message is repeated. Case in point—the telephone game. By the time the message is relayed between a number of individuals, it often has discrepancies that are stark in comparison to the original message.

"As it is written . . . so shall it be done" conjures up the vision of Ramses giving the order to put his decision in stone to ensure it is carried out. But will it be? Back then, it better have been carried out or you were likely to be greasing the stones as they built the next pyramid.

Today, however, you might just find yourself answering to those you report to as to why a budget was exceeded, an operational breakdown occurred, a project failed, or a goal was not reached. Depending on the severity or the frequency, it could lead to disciplinary measures or even termination.

Words are powerful and important in passing on instruction of any kind. Again you need to start with clarity. When we reduce our directives or decisions to writing, we expect our directives to be carried out with explicit adherence to the decisions that formed them. Once written, it is memorialized. However, if it is poorly interpreted, it is poorly written. That is why written communication carries so much weight, whether it be in the form of a memo (internal) or letter (external) or a contract that binds the terms we live with or a law that dictates what we can and cannot do and even determines how we do things. Laws become laws once they are codified, organized, and arranged with order into a systematic code (written).

Listening is critical in the discussion, debate, and hearing stages. Lack of listening skills can absolutely lead to bad outcomes in any of these cases. I often remind people we should not write policies in our companies or create ordinances in our communities that we cannot enforce. Often in the discussion phase, good reasoning supports logic for arguments that demand amendments or changes in the language that we are considering. If we fail to hear and understand the implications of those arguments, we could miss this opportunity and suffer the results.

In order for the listening to happen, the reader in this case must understand without question what is expected, prohibited, or acceptable. This can range from procedure to policy or from ordinances to laws. Companies have charters and bylaws to aid in understanding the policies and procedures that govern everything from acceptable behavior to how the business of that company is carried out.

This permeates our culture in interests that span more than just business, such as the arts and sports. Take classical music for instance. Verdi helped codify an international operatic culture in support of Italy's independence. "Born alongside Italy's press for nationhood, Verdi's operas provided Italians with the music that expressed the passion for their cause and became an important part of Italy's national identity."[1]

"In the 18th century, the Italian peninsula was fractured into parts controlled by different nations. A century later, the notion of a united Italy had evolved into a battle for independence, pitting Italy's revolutionaries against the might of Austria and the Papal States. Although soldiers and statesmen played a key role in what unfolded, Giuseppe Verdi's music provided the soundtrack to the desire for independence. Through his many works, Verdi reflected, and even shaped, the struggle for Italian unification known as Il

Risorgimento: the Resurgence."[2] His words permeated throughout the countryside to articulate the views of a people who wanted independence and needed the freedom and sovereignty of a nation.

Oral language, syntax, and sentence complexity are key in ensuring that what is written is understood not only by the writer, in this case the speaker or speakers if coauthored, but that it stands the test of time and that it has the ability to be understood by anyone who reads it, or in this case the listener. Speaking and listening through writing is how our nations are governed, terms and conditions are carried out and applied in business, and operations and practices are managed in companies. Speak clearly and exactingly and your instructions are understood and hopefully followed; write clearly and precisely and your instructions are understood and hopefully followed. The critical component rests with syntax and complexity. The degree of complexity follows the degree of complexity.

Common sense (coined by Thomas Paine)[3] dictates that a basic issue like distribution of supplies requires less complex wording to ensure understanding of the resolution or disposition than say a noncompete or nonsolicitation agreement restricting an individual from soliciting current or former clients of a company or business after leaving the business. This happens often after companies are taken over and senior sales agents of the former company decide to strike out on their own. Regardless of why an employee leaves, the separation in this scenario dictates a noncompete agreement. These agreements can include complex language designed to consider all aspects of what might arise in order to protect the company's customer base. The language can be part of a separate document or incorporated as a clause in an employment agreement covered upon hiring.

Avoiding poor decisions goes beyond those we might make to include those potentially made by the people in our charge. Why is this important as a manager or leader of individuals or teams? Because in order to avoid poor decisions by those in your charge, you must start with understanding the importance of how they listen and what they hear when processing those commands, orders, or instructions. A feedback mechanism such as a follow-up meeting or meetings to discuss the information or initiative or site visitation to observe the implementation firsthand allows you to gauge this. Equally, you have the same responsibility in processing information you are given. That is why the written explanations and instructions we author carry such importance.

The basic elements of any written material needed to convey information effectively must be centered on the 5 Ws: Who? What? When? Where? and Why? and sometimes How? or 5W1H. Figure 6.1 depicts the basic elements needed to effectively convey information.

"Who" is determined by your audience. It can be as large as the market, field, or industry if authoring an article or writing procedures or guidelines or

Figure 6.1.   Basic Elements Needed to Effectively Convey Information. *Source: Däv Dickenson, http://livingqlikview.com/five-ws-one-h/*

as small as a group of individuals within your company or organization if providing guidance or instruction. This matters and has an impact on the tone and technical level of the wording or how it is structured in the message (syntax). Knowing the "who" allows for the appropriate word choice to ensure that the message is processed and acted upon in the way in which it was written (back to Ramses).

"What" is the subject. It serves as a pronoun, asking for specific information; as a determiner, to provide that information; or an adverb, qualifying that information. Powerful and important, it covers the issue(s) to be considered or an incident that has already taken place and must now be dealt with. "What" is at the center of intent in any writing; it is the very reason that we are writing in the first place. Clarity and brevity are necessary to ensure that the reader gets and understands the message in the quickest, most practical manner. Think about the difference between memos, letters, reports, bulletins, pamphlets, articles, and books. They are determined for use by the "who" and "what." They are all technical writing instruments designed to promote understanding through conveyance of knowledge, fact, direction, disposition, policies, protocols, and procedures. The appropriate technical writing instrument will be determined by the breadth and depth of the information that needs to be shared. A bulletin, referring to a short official statement or broadcast, is a great example of everyday events put out in writing for consumption or presentation, as in headline news. Its purpose and intent is to distribute the message via a news flash in a communique or press release sharing the quick facts about the "what."

Could you imagine reading an eighty-page memo or flipping through a ten-page book? The memo would lose its point after the first page, and any book that concludes on a topic in ten pages is not very deep, and thus not a trusted or credible source. Either way you will lose the reader and fail to convey what is needed to make the appropriate decision or take the suitable action. In disciplinary actions the "what" covers much ground, as it addresses all three aspects (pronoun, determiner, and adverb).

"When" provides the timeline for the subject. It is the past, present, and future of events. It is as specific as it needs to be, and it needs to be specific based on "what" we are talking about. An injury, accident, or weather event, for instance, requires the importance of not only day, but time of day. In these circumstances, someone is filling out a report following the event. Details provide the essence of the event and capture the facts that allow us to gauge the import of the event and provide the necessary information to ensure appropriate understanding as to "what" took place. When preparing an incident report, provide the information in a brief memo (brevity) and employ the 5W1H principle to ensure understanding (clarity).

"When" has the power of urgency or the subtleness of preparation depending on "how" it is used, and it too determines the technical writing instrument that will best fit the bill. In the case of a disciplinary write-up, "when" requires us to know the date and time the event took place as it has relevance regarding the circumstances of "what" took place and whether this was a one-off or part of a pattern of behavior. It becomes a crucial step in recording progressive discipline that will support the actions taken and become part of the company's support or defense if the matter turns legal. If poorly written, or worse, not written at all, the organization can find themselves ill-prepared to defend the action against a wrongful termination suit.

Everything that is written should be done so with the thought that it will find its way to the courtroom as exhibit A. Prior to releasing important documents, you need to read and reread them and have a colleague check the documents for their understanding. I do this on important matters with my secretary, my assistant, other cabinet members, our CEO, and technical experts depending on the subject matter and the importance of recording it. This is how keen executives stay ahead of potential issues. If it is something with legal ramifications, have your legal team review it based on legal authority and soundness. Perceived savings on legal bills by avoiding this step may lead to massive payouts in settlements or judgments later. Absent this step we preclude our ability to listen to good advice and avoidance of poor decisions.

Keep in mind, once it is written, it is evidence. In the public sector in New Jersey, for example, it becomes a public document and as such is subject to copy requests from the public under the provision of the OPRA.[4] In New York you can gain access to contracts from public to vendors in a few clicks on the website www.seethroughny.net as part of their "See Through NY" program to promote transparency. Transparency and openness have become commonplace in today's society and place more responsibility on those composing these documents, contracts, and other instruments. Strict adherence to these principles (5W1H) allows one to write about or record the matter in a concise manner that remains succinct. This applies to another form of writing mostly overlooked, emails. The *e* in email stands for *evidence*—it can and will be seized in discovery and used against you and your organization if it helps the plaintiff.

"Where" provides location information. It allows the reader to focus on the point of occurrence or explain the appropriate or approved setting, site, or whereabouts that the "what" either took place or is scheduled to take place in relationship to the "when." Again the extent and detail of the "where" relies on the importance of the event or issue being referenced. In military actions or exercises this element is crucial and may need to be pinpointed with precise accuracy such as grid coordinates. In an incident report it may only require a particular site location. In these examples we describe "where" as at, in, or to which to reference a place or situation. It designates the position, direction, and circumstances of where the action is to take place or where it occurred—very important to providing a complete picture and confirming, certifying, or authorizing the necessary action.

"Why" provides the rationale or explanation for the "what." It is so important that a book was written about it as a key element in any company's success by Simon Sinek: *Start with Why: How Great Leaders Inspire Everyone to Take Action.*[5] Without the "why" we lack purpose and the importance of "what." As leaders we need to inspire those around us to do not just what is asked or expected, but to accomplish goals and objectives that require effort, motivation, trust, and extension of themselves or stretching. This is how we grow and achieve the impossible only to find it is doable. Absent the why, we fall short of desire and begin to question the effort.

In 1982 I reported to Fort Gordon, Georgia, for four months of AIT (advanced individual training) with the Signal Corps. The base had a simple motto, "CAN-DO," referring to any challenge that we encountered during our time there. It became such a part of our identity that it stayed with us even after we left to go on to our next assignments. What impressed me then and has stayed with me as a leader outside of the military was how it lent itself to every challenge or encounter beyond the military. Serving in the army, we got the "why" to protect our nation, but now we received reinforcement of the "how" in these two simple words, because we can . . . that is, do it . . . whatever it is!

That's the kind of inspiration we need to instill in our people. This comes from ensuring that the "why" is understood. Sinek covers this in his "golden circle": "Very few organizations know WHY they do what they do." "WHY is not about making money." "That's a result." "WHY is a purpose, cause or belief." "It's the very reason your organization exists."[6] Simple concept, powerful book.

The "why" in our written and oral instructions cements the reason for why something is done and validates the effort.

Ever had to complete a task or small job you didn't particularly care for or wished you could hand off to someone else in the company? Then someone explained the reason, need, or value in accomplishing this task or job and somehow it seemed less unappealing or at least understandable. Now consider the change in attitude and therefore effort while attacking the task or job with a renewed energy or vigor. The difference is purpose!

"Why" is purpose and meaning. Another such book that comes to mind is *The Purpose Driven Life*[7] by Rick Warren. The book deals with the basic question, why am I here? What is my purpose? While Warren's questions are rooted in our relationship with God, the concept is similar to Sinek's question regarding our relationship with our organization. Both require an answer to "why" in order to flourish in that relationship. So what is the tie-in to our purpose of avoiding poor decision-making through effective listening? How does the "why" factor into avoiding the "fist on the eye"? It is the parallels in meaning that stress the importance of the question. If we fail to understand the "why" in our own circumstance, how can we convey it to others? You must have a clear understanding of your organization's mission and how you fit into that undertaking before you can lead others in a way that mirrors or achieves that mission. Lacking this understanding will undoubtedly lead to miscommunicating the "why" and getting it wrong.

"How"—about that. . . . This one is pretty self-explanatory; it is all about the action, ways, and means. In what manner should we accomplish what is needed? But be sure to provide explicit direction to ensure you get the results you are looking for. Deviations could produce a different outcome and one that is not in line with your expectations. As a supervisor or administrator, writing skills are so important in conveying and recording actions, yet often individuals who exhibit poor performance are left to muddle through due to passive or ineffective evaluations. This symptom of ineffective operational performance by a group, team, or division of an organization will only worsen over time without immediate action that includes training on preparation of effective evaluations, or removal of the ineffective manager/supervisor/administrator. Take the case of "The Shining Star."

A building principal once asked for my help in dealing with a head custodian that had all but worn this principal out, and she wanted him gone. I sat in her office and listened to the current issues as well as past transgressions that summed up one point—it was time for a change, and this individual needed to go! New to the district, I lacked the history and detailed knowledge of the staff and had to rely on the few observations I made, which started with the state of the building, which was lacking. Corridors were dark and dingy, showing old faded paint, dust, dirt, and grime marks from years of wax buildup at the base. Classrooms weren't much better, with missing or broken ceiling tiles, scuffed-up floors, and dirty windows. The windows actually had buildup and had started to become cloudy. The grounds demonstrated the same picture of neglect.

OK, so this should be an easy fix, I told her. Then I asked to see his evaluations both current and past. Uh-oh, "Houston we have a problem."

The evaluations were all over the place and inconsistent with the observable facts that led to the discussion. In one evaluation she wrote, "I am so disappointed in your performance today; however, I know you can be the best of the best and I have witnessed this on many occasions." In another one that put the brakes on the quick fix, she referred to him as the "shining star" that kept the building running like a "miracle worker." These inconsistencies provided a series of mixed reactions and claims both positive and negative in the narrative sections of the evaluations. The evaluations on the whole were more flattering or positive than the few negatives over the years; however, the state of the building and grounds did not match the positive statements. I looked her straight in the eye and said, "I cannot make a case for pulling this individual at this time due to a lack of progressive discipline." The evaluations painted a different picture and would only work in his favor should we decide to move forward with any reassignment or termination at this time. Instead of admonishing her for the lack of meaningful evaluations, I counseled her on the appropriate use and steps and importance of progressive discipline.

I further explained that when used properly, it can serve as an effective method to provide notice to employees who are not meeting expected or communicated job performance standards, exhibiting behaviors that are unacceptable, or violating policies and procedures. The intent is not to move to dismissal but to help employees correct their issue(s) and become successful and productive. While this is the intended use, it requires effort by the employee, and if not corrected could lead to termination of employment. I concluded by stating that separation is our last resort, as we have already invested in the individuals upon hiring.

When it comes to evaluating personnel, be honest, up-front, direct, and to the point. Avoiding honesty diminishes the intent of the evaluation and renders it worthless, as in the case above with the head custodian and the principal. Dressing it up only masks the truth and allows the poor performance to continue. Regardless of how unpleasant it is to hold individuals accountable and administer discipline, it is required of good leaders and beneficial to the individual as well as the organization.

Evaluations are about three things—the good, the bad, and the ugly. Dress it up too much and you become the problem. Good leadership means doing the right thing all the time, even when it is not the easy or in this case the pleasant thing.

Do not exaggerate or sugarcoat it. Evaluations are effective tools that are designed to improve performance by identifying strengths and weakness and targeting areas for improvement. In order for the evaluation to have merit, it must accurately reflect the actions taken during the performance period. It is that simple. Avoid common mistakes that stray from the intent of effective evaluations.

Five Common Mistakes That Compromise Evaluations:

1. *Piling on*—Continuous reprimand of prior-period issues. This should be avoided unless they are reoccurring in the current period. Otherwise it creates a "prison feel" or "purgatory" and you will lose credibility with the member and team, as they will begin to feel for the wronged and overlook wrongdoings.
2. *Dressing up*—Making the evaluation appear better than the actual performance displayed to protect the evaluated and the evaluator from embarrassment. "Putting lipstick on that pig!"
3. *Single focus*—An evaluation must be concerned with the entire period, not the first or last thirty days, and representative of the entire period. We can see improvement or decline within this period and as such it must be noted. Similarly, we can see recovery and improvement after a verbal counseling or write-up. This must be given equal weight as we ultimately seek to improve performance and enhance our investment in human capital. Strong employee performance is beneficial to all parties and our ultimate aim.
4. *Vengeance*—Curb your emotions and stick to the facts. Clear objectivity maintains professionalism and gets your point across. Stay fair and honest even if the evaluation is bad. Do not make it personal or misuse it to seek revenge. Avoid the three Rs: retaliation, retribution, or reprisal.
5. *Time lapse*—Late or missing periods in evaluations means you do not care or you are just going through the motions. In order to make them matter, they must be timely. When done at proper intervals monthly,

quarterly, or annually, they serve to reinforce good behavior and allow top performers to be validated.

The best way to manage evaluations is to work on them throughout the time period by jotting down notes or recording incidents via electronic aids such as smartphone apps or minirecorders that can serve as memory aids later.

Evaluations are not always easy, but consider the harm you do to yourself and others when you let behaviors that are unacceptable continue. The harmful effects will spread to the rest of your group and create an environment that is contrary to trust, openness, and effective listening.

Takeaway: think before you write.

Chapter Seven

Word Choice and Use

How to Get Your Point Across Effectively

Word choice is one of the most important decisions you make as a speaker. It colors the discussion and determines the feel or mood of your audience. Choose the right words and it can foster a climate of trust, pride, partnership, and closeness. Choose the wrong words and it can incite panic, distrust, embarrassment, and separation. Getting your point across effectively requires the help of the appropriate word choice to explain, support, and tailor the message in a way that is warmly received. People generally do not listen once the message goes against their sensitivities. Misunderstandings stem from poor communications that lead in many cases to the wrong decision or action.

Some of the worst word choices are embedded in familiar phrases that hamper our listening as the communications become one-way—from the listener to the speaker instead of a conversation. We have all experienced individuals who hijack the conversation by throwing out words such as "I know," "oh yeah," or "right," and then they shift the focus to themselves, thus short-circuiting the speaker. One killer word to any conversation is "but": That's nice—"but"; stop at *nice* or whatever compliment, agreement, or reinforcing word is used and allow the person talking to know you are listening. Once you throw in the "but," you are just hijacking the conversation to steer it back to you, your experiences, or your thoughts.

Tact and humility are equally important in addressing issues that impact others, regardless of the importance of the message.

How you get your point across is determined by these three things: tone, messaging, and word choice.

1. Tone—How you talk to people
2. Messaging—What you talk about
3. Word choice—How you deliver the message effectively

TONE

The aim of well-chosen wording is to ensure that what is written or spoken is correctly understood in the best light. It's all about feeling. "The tone makes the music" is a phrase I took from my wife and have been applying for years in counseling staff, colleagues, and others. It gets the message across immediately, as it reminds us to dial back the aggression that comes from aggravation, disappointment, frustration, or annoyance with difficulties that arise or those who fall short of accomplishing tasks. When we need to get the team back on track, we can holler at them, berate them, or just threaten them and see how things improve—my guess is they will do worse depending on the group, scenario, or circumstance. Do a Google search on the following topic—harmful effects of berating staff—and see what pops up (see figure 7.1).

Articles like these underscore the effects of job performance in relationship to workplace bullying. This does not say that as a manager or leader you will never raise your voice or challenge those around you to reach deeper or think of a better way by yelling. Yelling and berating are two different issues and as such need to be considered separately. While berating has no benefits and should never happen, depending on the culture and climate of your organization, yelling may not only work at times, it may be expected.

Think back to the sports competitive environment and the coaches; think they yell? What goes in the pros may not fly where you work—or will it? I came across an interesting article in the *Harvard Business Review* titled "Is It OK to Yell at Your Employees?" and the answer was yes! As quoted from the article, "To be sure, yelling doesn't make someone a better leader or manager. But the notion that raising one's voice represents managerial weakness or a failure of leadership seems to be prima facie nonsense."[1] Think they ever yelled in the Army?

One of the best-known yellers was Bobby Knight, the legendary coach of the Indiana University Basketball Hoosiers. Knight won three national titles during his twenty-nine years at Indiana University. While he produced results, not everybody would want to be on that team, and after the chair-throwing incident in 1985, Indiana University did not want Knight on their team. Although he amassed a total of 902 wins in men's Division I Basketball by the time he retired in 2008, he was best remembered for the chair-throwing incident and his temper.

Tone changes based on character and attitude even with the musical association of the term with reference to its pitch, quality, and strength. In the

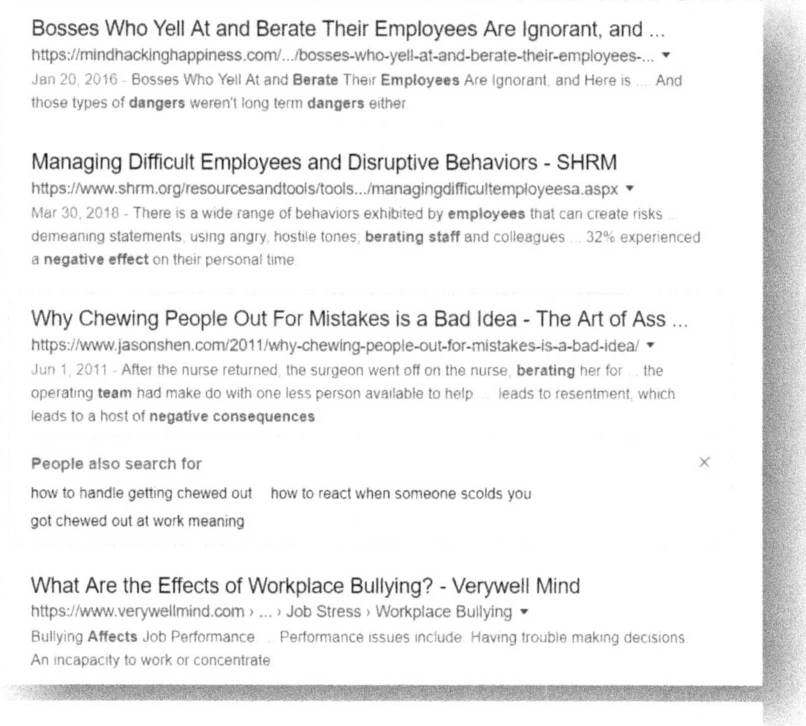

Figure 7.1. *Source: Google search*

situation of speaking or writing, the elements pitch and strength define the general character or mood. A stern tone and serious demeanor can have the same effect or even deeper impact in dealing with individuals than yelling at them.

Reminds me of learning the differences in leadership styles between McGregor's Theory X and Theory Y management styles in grad school.[2]

"If you believe that your team members dislike their work and have little motivation, then, based on McGregor's findings, you'll likely use an authoritarian style of management. This approach is very 'hands-on' and usually involves micromanaging people's work to ensure that it gets done properly. McGregor called this Theory X.

"On the other hand, if you believe that your people take pride in their work and see it as a challenge, then you'll more likely adopt a participative management style. Managers who use this approach trust their people to take ownership of their work and do it effectively by themselves. McGregor called this Theory Y."[3]

Theory X managers are often yellers, and I for one did not appreciate or respond to that type of approach. Likewise, my experience in the military was more of raised voices and shouting of commands or orders than getting constantly yelled at (other than basic training, but thank God that only lasted for two months). Outside of sports and military organizations one must consider whether yelling has a place in your organization's culture.

While I favor Theory Y and operate under this belief most of the time, I do believe Theory X has its place depending on the circumstances and what is at stake. The reality is most everything in business requires balance, for example, "work-life balance," in order to provide sustainable, productive, and motivated employees. I also believe in a balanced approach to McGregor's theory that more closely resembles two parts Y and one part X, or Y2X. I believe there are times when you alternate between grabbing the reins and then handing them back over to your team. I have found you need to be versatile enough in managing the differences in people on your team to know how to apply each strategy and to what degree based on the circumstances. You cannot run a business on warm, cuddly smiles—it's not practical and it's not reality based. There are individuals in organizations that are lazy and self-centered, lack ambition, dislike change, and long to be told what to do; most often these individuals are inherited or passed off through transfers from one fed-up manager to a new, unsuspecting manager as they even come "highly endorsed." These individuals need all the "X" you can muster. The real question is, why are they permitted to stay? As Collins, author of *Good to Great*,[4] puts it, you need to get them off the bus. Those same organizations have motivated people who take pride in their work and see it as a challenge, thus flourishing under a "Y" scenario.

Situational leadership requires "push and pull"; there are times to steer and times to simply watch the progress that is unfolding. The hybrid model "Y2X" allows variations of this approach. This proves effective when dealing with situations requiring swift action designed to avoid or mitigate the storm. It is indispensable when planning is critical and time allows for thoughtful planning and guidance. One style or approach to management assumes every situation is the same, and that's just not reality.

I am not alone in this, as written in a 2010 article titled "Theory U and Theory T" that appeared in the magazine *strategy+business* by Matthew Stewart, challenging the concept of only choice in style, X or Y.[5] "McGregor named his theories after letters . . . and he further insisted that both theories have value in the appropriate contexts."

In support of Theory Y, Stewart points out that "many managers and many firms took McGregor's message to heart and learned how to help themselves by helping their people flourish. The glittering pot of gold at the end of the Theory Y rainbow is in fact, now a commonplace, that many of the most successful companies in the world are routinely rated the best places to work."

He goes on to say, "We are all Theory Y people now—at least when it comes to delivering or receiving motivational talks—and yet, truth be told, we all have our doubts that the world has caught up with our wisdom about it. It will have already occurred to many people, for example, that quite a few of those companies are great places to work because they are successful, rather than the other way around." "There is also plenty of anecdotal evidence to suggest that firms change their assumptions about human nature after their fortunes change, rather than before."

Employees are resources, but they are first human. Nobody wants to get screamed at, but that doesn't mean they should get a free pass when they violate policy or exhibit poor performance. Instead we can be up-front, honest, and truthful in speaking to them and working together to overcome the obstacles or change behaviors. Someone close to me once said, "I'm a nice guy and I always smile . . . but when it is necessary I tell my people—Don't mistake my kindness for weakness." Well put, Doug.

Encouragement is the way to foster an environment of trust and confidence in making progress. Accountability is the tool that keeps people moving in the right direction. Strength of honesty is what binds these two items together. Honesty is at the core of trust that makes the Theory Y2X a functional hybrid that works based on today's realities in the workplace. This theory is supported by the work of Stephen Covey and R. R. Merrill[6] regarding trust and Jim Collins[7] regarding accountability.

We all suffer setbacks from time to time in any organization, especially when accomplishing difficult tasks requiring significant time and effort along with a high degree of skill. Trial and error is key in solving new problems that are untested or difficult. Making mistakes means we are attempting to solve, and yet we are learning what doesn't work or ruling out various aspects of those attempts.

MESSAGING

Messaging is all about word choice and crafting the right message. It requires laying out those words in the best way to achieve the understanding you are looking for. Organizations hire PR firms to accomplish just that on a large scale. Outwardly, our messages serve to promote our values, principles, and success in a way that bolsters our stock. The same care that goes into protecting our brand, reputation, and identity needs to permeate throughout the organization to every manager who shares in that responsibility.

Think big "external"—try thinking small "internal." Inwardly, our messages serve to instill our values, beliefs, and goals in a way that aligns our actions with our mission. Every time you engage with your team members, you have an opportunity to incorporate that vision into your messaging to share the mission with those you lead. Do it right and they become part of the mission in a way that transcends their job and becomes part of a shared identity that solidifies the brand. They become spokespersons for the organization within the organization and serve as ambassadors every time they travel outside the organization.

A story that captures the heart of this concept is one Jeff McCausland, founder and CEO of Diamond6, likes to tell about a NASA janitor and JFK. In 1962, President John F. Kennedy visited NASA for the first time. During his tour of the facility, he met a janitor who was carrying a broom down the hallway. The president then casually asked the janitor what he did for NASA, and the janitor replied, "I'm helping put a man on the moon." The janitor got it. He understood the vision, his part in it, and he had purpose.

Individuals are identified as part of the company when we see that company's logo on their business cards, clothing, or ID badges. This ties them to the brand as an asset, and they are . . . or are they a liability? Messaging reinforces the expectations of acceptable behavior, acceptable dress, and acceptable travel. These items are generally covered in memos, employee handbooks, or even state and federal regulations if considered a public employee. Every time your members converse with other colleagues in professional settings, they evoke messaging to get your point across or just "talk to talk" absent any real thought or care. If they begin to depart from the company's philosophy or represent themselves in a way less than professional, they become a liability to the organization.

So how do we instill the need to improve overall communication skills with our employees? Start by incorporating communications into your professional development. PD opportunities provide another forum to articulate the goals of the company in a way that promotes team concepts.

There are plenty of online resources and activities to assist you in planning group activities that target these skills. Following are some free training activities that focus on specific key communication skills:

Communication Origami

This is a quick and easy activity that shows how the same instructions are interpreted differently by different people and highlights the importance of clear communication.

The Guessing Game

This simple activity is a fun way to introduce and show the difference between closed and open questions.

Guess the Emotion

This is a fun competitive game that's concerned with getting participants to become more aware of their feelings or emotions. Participants are split into teams and act out an emotion, such as disgust, affection, fear, anxiety, embarrassment, anger, or determination.

Power of Body Language

Body language speaks louder than any words you can ever utter. Whether you're telling people that you love them, you're angry with them, or don't care less about them, your body movements reveal your thoughts, moods, and attitudes. Both consciously and subconsciously your body tells others what's really going on with you. This is a great, quick, and fun activity that shows how powerful the effect of body language is in communicating with others.

Follow All Instructions Activity

This is a quick, fun activity with a little trick to see how many of the participants will actively listen and follow the one single instruction you will give them, "Read all instructions first," and how many will rush and start doing each instruction one by one.

Effective Feedback Skill Practice Exercise

An overview of effective and ineffective feedback and a good activity for practicing giving effective feedback.

The Name Game

Instruct each participant to think of a famous person and write it secretly on a Post-it note. Attach the note to the head of their partner. A fun exercise that shows the importance of asking the right type of questions.

Square Talk

This is a challenging activity where participants are all blindfolded and receive instructions from the trainer that should be strictly followed. The exercise enables participants to recognize the importance of communicating effectively and understand the important aspects of communication.

Room 101

The purpose of this exercise is to practice your influential and persuasive skills in a competitive, fun debate focusing on communication skills like choosing positive language, being passionate and enthusiastic about one's case, showing "benefits" to others, and so forth.

Back-to-Back Communication

A classic communication skills activity that highlights the importance of asking questions for effective communication.

We have opportunities each time we send out a memo, prepare in-house trainings, lead team discussions, or recognize staff. Well-crafted messages ensure understanding and buy-in that promotes value, commitment, and pride in what they do and where they come from. This is true of opportunities to present on relevant topics in your field or when they engage in professional settings that tie back to the company's success in developing and supporting their knowledge and efforts.

What I'm saying is, you can have a big impact in the little things you do through quality messaging. Regardless of the audience, a well-crafted message plays at any speed from media contacts to the boardroom to current or prospective employees. The time spent crafting these written instruments ensures our core messages are bulletproof, easy to understand, and translatable in any format or any venue.

WORD CHOICE

Our words carry power in the affirmation of what we believe and value. Our thoughts come to life as we speak the words that impact our lives personally and professionally. It is our words that lay the foundation of any understanding as they reveal our intentions. They are a confirmation to those outside the organization of how we see things both as they are and how they should be, which broadcasts our vision. It is the powerful affirmation that our words provide that allows our thoughts to be transformed into a reality.

Word choice is what allows us to effectively deliver the message. Our message will live or die by the words we use. Words have both positive and negative connotations. They evoke emotions and stir up sentiment that can be for or against us or what we are selling. We must ensure that we grab the right ones to achieve our objective of understanding and avoidance of poor decisions.

If we do not "make the case" through our words, our advice or counsel can go unheeded, and with that we could lose the whole ship—that is, the *Titanic*. Even the name affirmed its power and invincibility. It was unsinkable . . . and yet it sank. *Titanic* received six warnings of sea ice on April 14 but was traveling near her maximum speed when her lookouts sighted the iceberg.

We need to use words that are closer in meaning to the actual events we are speaking to.

If I had the reports and was briefing Captain Smith, I'd be using words like imminent threat, immediate danger, disastrous consequences, and life and death.

When it comes to health and safety, we must be forceful and direct without hesitation or intimidation of rank. Good leaders want "real information" in "real time." Anything less and you are losing time that could be better spent in mitigation, activation, or termination of an action as simple as let's change course. A poor choice of words is those that water down the message by diluting the urgency, thus delaying the action. Smart managers understand that time-sensitive material needs to "get eyes on it" while it has value. The value depreciates rapidly the longer you hold it. Wait too long and the information is worthless as the time to act is over.

In the same way ships look to avoid icebergs, managers look to avoid problems and exposure (legal, personal, insurance). Avoidance of negative words helps us sidestep potentially damaging situations or better yet refrain from exacerbating an already bad situation. This rationale is fundamental at the top levels of any organization in deciding how to address the press during any situation. Keep in mind, they are looking for a story, and any misstep on your part will increase the "type set" or character font size of the headline.

Icebergs come in all shapes and sizes, just as the issues companies and organizations face on an ongoing basis. Navigating these waters can prove challenging as well. Some issues appear small, but keep in mind over 90 percent of an iceberg's volume (and mass) is underwater. This is where getting out ahead of the problem or issue is key to having control of the situation and message. Although a problem may exist, it will only get larger and eventually grow beyond your scope to contain and address any meaningful fix.

Once you become aware—you become responsible.

The best advice I give when counseling supervisors and managers as well as staff regarding this is—Once you become aware, you become responsible. This is the point of decision where listening is crucial, as it is often those who report to you that are informing you of the issue. Ignoring the message is the same as failing to listen and will lead to a poor decision.

Not only do we need to choose the right words, we must be timely about it.

Oftentimes managers overanalyze the problem while trying to craft the perfect response, resulting in "paralysis through analysis." This brings with it additional damage to the company or organization as they are seen as weak, inept, or uncompromising. Even when they get the message out, it can come across as a reactionary move and put the group in a less-than-perfect light. Sometimes they just bungle, mishandle, or mismanage the situation.

The following examples are a few high-profile companies that mishandled situations due to their inability or refusal to listen:[8]

Bridgestone Tire Debacle (2000)[9]

Bridgestone began receiving complaints about their Firestone tires treads' tendency to separate, often resulting in horrific accidents, starting in 1998.

But they refused to admit that there was a real problem until 2000, when the NHTSA launched a large-scale investigation. After much waffling in the press, Bridgestone finally accepted blame, and on August 9, 2000, they announced the recall of 6.5 million tires—the second-largest recall in US history.

Merck Recalls Vioxx (2004)[10]

Even though preliminary studies in 2000 had suggested that the painkiller Vioxx posed a potential heart health risk, executives at pharmaceutical giant Merck chose not to pursue those studies further.

Four years later, Merck was forced to recall that very drug because of evidence that it may have caused heart attacks and cardiac deaths in thousands of its users. The recall turned into a massive scandal as reports came out that Merck had known about the serious risk yet continued to promote the drug anyway.

The company faced an SEC investigation and hundreds of lawsuits as a result of its actions. The scandal was finally laid to rest in 2009, as reported by the *Wall Street Journal*, when Merck settled litigation for $80 million.

JetBlue Traps Passengers on the Runway for Hours (2007)[11]

In early 2007, nine JetBlue flights at JFK airport were delayed for up to eleven hours because of serious inclement weather. Normally, this wouldn't have resulted in much more than a few really irritated travelers, but in this case, JetBlue decided to keep its nearly one thousand passengers trapped in the runway-bound planes for the entire time.

CBS News reported passengers described the experience as "horrific." As snacks depleted and the bathroom situation grew unpleasant, people on the planes grew more and more upset that they were not being allowed to deplane and just walk to the terminal, which was within sight. They were only permitted to leave the aircrafts when official airport vehicles finally arrived to transport them.

JetBlue at first defended its decision, arguing that its passengers' safety in the ice storm was top priority, but the incident sparked government debate about passengers' rights. According to Consumer Affairs, a week later, Jet-Blue announced its own "Passengers' Bill of Rights," which detailed different levels of compensation for varying types of delays, as well as a promise to deplane passengers after five hours' delay in the future.

These are just a few well-publicized situations in which poor decisions were made absent effective listening, as I am sure in each case somebody was providing "real information in real time" that was obviously ignored. Could these disasters have been averted through better word choice in sounding the alarm? Proper word choice in these examples, as with the *Titanic*, would have led to better choices and quicker realization of what was ultimately at stake. In the case of Bridgestone and Merck, it was clearly lives and money; however, all three took a hit regarding the company's reputation.

The same holds true for solving problems with your groups, teams, sections, or divisions within the organization. Rethink your vocabulary and work to avoid bad word choices by inserting more productive words that strengthen your image and promote your culture. Here are a couple examples that I use regularly in dealing with staff, directors, board members, and the public:

Concerns instead of complaints—If individuals take the time to contact us, they have a concern and need to be heard. Labeling it as a complaint starts us down the negative path to avoidance and defensive posturing.

Opportunities instead of problems—True, we all encounter problems; however, with a positive attitude and open mind we can see them as opportunities to make needed changes within any organization.

Optimism instead of pessimism—A brighter outlook allows for flexibility and opens creativity to gain a fresh perspective regarding any issue.

The most common negative words that prevent us from achieving results are *no* and *not*. Other negative words include *neither, never, no one, nobody, none, nor, nothing, nowhere*. These words evoke the emotions of helplessness, defeat, aggravation, annoyance, and anger. When someone has come to you with a concern, work to avoid making it into a complaint, and you are on the road to turning it into a resolution. Even when people do not get exactly what they want, they walk away much more satisfied knowing they were heard and understood. That is not going to happen when the first word out of your mouth is *no*.

So how do we select the positive words and avoid the negative words to improve reception of our message? Focus on the positive aspects and avoid negativity while drafting the message. Writing a memo or addressing a situation when it is "too fresh" or "raw" opens the reservoir of negative words that fit our mood and seem to express our sentiments perfectly. They probably do . . . at that moment; however, are they the best choice of words to correct the behavior in question? Or will they simply lead to a deeper divide and separation that results in a poor decision on your part and a skewed perspective on their part? I have seen situations where employees have been reprimanded in such a harsh manner that it negates the message, and the opportunity for corrective action is lost as they now become recalcitrant.

Instead take the advice I was given a long time ago: put the draft away for a day and revisit it, as the words chosen may need be changed.

Chapter Eight

Thinking Together

Extending Meaning through Discussion

"Think tank" is a term that dates back to World War II, adopted by the military as a "safe place" to plan, strategize, and have open discussion. The meaning evolved in the 1960s as nonprofit policy research organizations began to adopt the model as a way to think outside the box. The purpose of these think factories or policy institute centers was to perform research on a host of topics in a way that maximized the thought process, thus returning superior findings. Some think tanks, such as the Brookings Institution or the Heritage Foundation, have become household names and are cited frequently by major news corporations. These are a few of the top think tanks in the United States:

- Brookings Institution
- Center for Strategic and International Studies
- Carnegie Endowment for International Peace
- Heritage Foundation
- Woodrow Wilson International Center for Scholars
- RAND Corporation
- Center for American Progress (CAP)
- Council on Foreign Relations (CFR)

What they have in common is some of the brightest minds available to research, discuss, and comment on issues too important and intricate for one person alone to ponder. Talk about strength in numbers, these folks deliver with as much as $7.7 M in monthly volume in the case of the Belfer Center for Science and International Affairs.[1]

"With offices in New York City and Washington, DC, the Council on Foreign Relations (CFR) is considered by some to be the most influential foreign-policy think tank in the United States. Including names like Fareed Zakaria, Colin Powell, Tom Brokaw, and Madeleine Albright, CFR's impressive membership list has included senior politicians, more than a dozen Secretaries of State, CIA directors, bankers, lawyers, professors, and prominent media figures. CFR is perhaps best known by the general public as the publisher of the widely read bi-monthly journal *Foreign Affairs*. In policy circles, however, CFR is known for its 'David Rockefeller Studies Program,' which often succeeds in influencing foreign policy by making official recommendations to the president and diplomatic community, testifying before Congress, speaking with the media, and publishing on issues of foreign policy."[2]

So what do we have in common with these think tanks? The ability to assemble some of the brightest minds in our own organizations, communities, and regions? Thinking "outside the box" sometimes means thinking "outside the organization." Working together as a think tank gives us better opportunity to gain deeper insights and other perspectives.

In education we share best practices with colleagues from other districts across the state and across the country. In working to better protect students and staff, top districts meet with police representatives from neighboring communities in addition to our own. They attend trainings with local and state police, the Department of Homeland Security, and some have even traveled to the FEMA institute in Emmitsburg, Maryland. All this is in recognition of one hard fact—working together as a think tank gives them opportunity to gain deeper insights and other perspectives that, if they are listening, can help to avoid poor decisions in their districts, and those decisions can save lives.

Organizations need to maintain open lines of communication within the organization to foster more opportunities to brainstorm or think more broadly by putting think tank models into practice. Focusing on career bands and career levels, we have both opportunity and structure. Bands within an organization make sense for a variety of reasons, starting with the shared functionality of the group—for example, supervisory/management band. This band would include all supervisors regardless of the department or area they supervise. Their shared responsibilities of managing employees, implementing goals, establishing objectives, managing budgets, and deploying resources make them a perfect match to research, troubleshoot, and solve problems they encounter within their departments. The commonalities in their respective responsibilities would provide ample opportunities to share what works as well as seek improvements from the larger brain trust. Webster's describes it as "a group of official or unofficial advisers concerned especially with planning and strategy."[3] The key word—advisers. The key act—listening.

Organizational charts provide a map of the organization denoting support positions and direct lines connecting bands within the structure to directors and executives responsible for achieving the goals of the organization. It creates a clear visual depiction of the hierarchy and departments that make up the organization. This map shows how information flows between levels within the company.

When creating think tanks or brainstorming, you need to look at stars at every level. These standouts provide perspectives that may otherwise go unheard, allowing an organization to miss out on critical information from "boots on the ground." This misstep could lead to poor decisions at the top.

While the executive level is a prestigious place within any organization as the seat of power, smart executives never lose their connection to the troops on the front lines, especially the line item commanders. These individuals can be found at the entry level with the lion's share of staff responsibilities. It is these individuals who carry out the plans of the organization through the daily accomplishment of tasks. Want some immediate "feedback," spend some time with them, even if it's a quick walk-through or an occasional lunch.

This is difficult at times because once team members feel they are able to speak freely, you may not like what they have to say. On the flip side, it allows you to stay on top of small matters before they become large ones, thus providing a better chance of avoiding deadly icebergs.

If you want the feedback to be open and honest, operate under the guides of "no reprisals." Trust me, it is more difficult than it sounds, and if you have been there you know; however, if you violate the trust to act immediately on small issues of disagreement or deviations in behavior, you compromise the supervisor and kill off future trust in open and honest communications. Remember, these frontline supervisors have their own relationships with the rank and file that require trust. Instead be a listener and apply the information gathered into positive adjustments or strategic planning to realign objectives with the organizational goals.

When it comes to honest feedback, most people focus on who said what. *Don't worry about who is saying what; focus on what is being said!*

Developing influential advisers or confidants within your department, organization, industry, or field is a smart way to stay in touch with the reality of your impact on the groups you manage and the arena you perform in. The importance of regular meetings within these groups is critical to maintaining stability, expectations and readiness, and knowledge.

Paramount to operational efficiency and management of your teams in any organization is having and utilizing appropriate meeting space conducive to the type of meeting planned. Whether it be flexible, bright, and open for creative brainstorming, or structured and accommodating for working sessions or presentations, you need to ensure that the space is properly equipped with high speed Wi-Fi, premium AV/IT equipment, or other needs such as production services or areas for refreshments. Proper setups and space offerings will allow for the "value" of information that is generated. Now all you need to do is listen, harvest that value, and then plan on how to act upon it.

Creating an environment of trust within your company starts with you. As a "trust broker," you need to model this behavior in your actions both up and down the chain of command. You need to be able to listen and provide an atmosphere of trust in allowing subordinates to speak, question, and provide insights from their perspective. Loyalty plays a big part in this, as it remains at the heart of trust for both parties. Absent that trust, you have no loyalty and the communication lines are severed.

The army defines this relationship as follows: "A loyal Soldier is one who supports the leadership and stands up for fellow Soldiers. By wearing the uniform of the U.S. Army you are expressing your loyalty. And by doing your share, you show your loyalty to your unit."[4]

This same support is found in successful companies and organizations when loyalty and trust are in place. Trust is critical to evaluations, feedback, direction, orders, commands, advisement, recommendations, and any other act that involves speaking and listening. Listening in a climate of trust allows the speaker to give honest assessments in an environment of professional feedback. Any leader who doesn't want to hear honest feedback is sure to encounter major difficulties and poor results. This pertains to both positive and negative feedback, as both are essential in managing and improving performance.

Keep in mind, while negative feedback is important for corrective action and long-term improvement, positive feedback is what drives us to succeed even bigger on a larger scale. For the motivated it is pure adrenaline, producing intense feelings of euphoria, happiness, and alertness. All great leaders want to do better; they want to continue to get the approval of their peers and whom they answer to. Overfocusing on negative feedback thwarts that progress and, absent appropriate praise, kills off the motivation.

This was proven in a study conducted by renowned business leaders Jack Zenger and Joe Folkman.[5] Using a series of psychometrically valid items, Zenger and Folkman created a self-assessment that measured a leader's preference for giving or avoiding the two basic kinds of feedback: positive feedback—defined as praise and reinforcement; and negative feedback, corrective—pointing out errors or missed opportunities.

Their study included a global sample of 8,671 leaders. The self-assessment revealed that 56 percent of the leaders had a stronger preference for giving negative feedback, 31 percent preferred giving positive feedback, while only 12 percent were equal in their preference. According to Folkman, the results begged the question, "Why do leaders prefer giving negative feedback despite describing it as more difficult to give than positive feedback?"[6] Perhaps because effective leaders understand the benefit and reasoning behind honest evaluations that, if used properly, provide the appropriate tool to recognize and reward good behavior while at the same time setting a course correction for unacceptable behaviors. It becomes a guide to illustrate clearly not only where the deficiencies are but, equally important, how to improve. Subsequent evaluations aid in measurements of the progress, thus becoming positive reinforcement.

Zenger and Folkman then posed a follow-up question to the sample group stating, "The best managers are those who deliver more praise and recognition than negative feedback." Only 33 percent of leaders who preferred giving negative feedback agreed with the statement, compared to 77 percent of those who preferred giving positive feedback.

Any feedback of value must originate with truth, honesty, and thoughtfulness. Truth in what is being observed is what is written into the evaluation as a record of performance, good or bad; honesty in addressing the strengths and weakness of the performance in relationship to the expectations and requirements of the job; and thoughtfulness regarding the intent of the actions that need to be improved and those of a positive nature that need to be maintained. In essence, evaluations are a time to celebrate the good things and address the concerns without losing the desire to serve the organization, the team, and ultimately the evaluator.

Giving high praise and recognizing good performance is not evidence of weakness in management, it is a sign of appreciation and good leadership. This type of recognition is meaningless if it is not earned or if it is undeserved. You don't want to hand out excellent ratings like Pez candy. It renders them meaningless and drives down performance from others, including those who receive the inflated scores. Further, it sets the bar of acceptable achievement lower.

Further, it should be noted that Zenger and Folkman's work demonstrated that leaders preferring to give negative feedback had an overall effectiveness rating at the thirty-fifth percentile, while those preferring to give positive feedback were at the forty-seventh percentile.[7]

Still feedback through evaluations is more one-on-one in the delivery; however, the evaluation process is one that requires broad-based support in its development, application, and implementation. As we opened the chapter talking about thinking together and extending meaning through discussion, the evaluation process fits nicely into this group thought process.

When working for agreement on any process or new procedure, it is important that those in the group speak out. This ensures that real agreement is reached and the process or procedure is accepted by those in the group, as they will be the ones to implement and uphold its application. As the leader of the discussion or session, you need to have a keen awareness of any silence or body language that implies dissatisfaction or lack of support, as this is often not voiced, especially among subordinates.

This also happens whenever someone voices objections or proposes modifications and is shot down as others decide to stay clear of the obvious unwelcomed comments. Instead we should welcome the comments and evaluate them for merit, as those in the room are sharing their thoughts and ideas and providing insights. That is the purpose of the group meeting. Unfortunately, the reality is we have all experienced those meetings where the group is assembled, the comments are requested, and the decision was made before the meeting even started. Not only does that turn off the team members, it sets the group back for future contributions and stops the exchange of information or knowledge swap.

Worse yet is when individuals in the group reach out to advise and assist based on their experience and skill set only to be brushed off. Good leaders understand this and accept counsel from those around them. Mentoring is founded on this principle and is meant to strengthen those new to leadership positions and those who aspire to leadership.

Recognizing good advice and what it looks like comes from gaining and accepting wisdom. It provides career assistance and helps us not only to see the obstacles in our path but to successfully navigate them. That is why we need to act on it.

When we analyze the makeup of high-level groups within organizations, we often find multiple mentors and protégés at the same table working to solve issues and provide operational guidance. With this much experience and expertise in the room it provides a golden opportunity to explore and expand on that knowledge base to reach optimal results. Thinking together allows the sharing of insights, thoughts, and creativity. Recognizing the value of mentoring ensures that those in the group are engaged, valued, and encouraged to participate in that process.

For this reason, mentoring is critical on our path to success not only as individuals but as companies or organizations. Studies have shown that mentor-protégé relationships provide psychosocial and instrumental career support for protégés. A cross-sectional survey showed that five distinct outcomes associated with mentor-protégé relationships are success, awareness, advancement, attitudes, and behaviors.[8] As with all instruction, mentoring is predicated on listening and applying the knowledge transferred from the mentor to the protégé.

The need for mentoring is predicated on advisement to ensure the success of young leaders. Mentoring is another form of leading, encouraging, or steering our career moves and decisions that ensure they have meaning and lasting impact. The benefits derived from mentoring stem from proven and effective ways to mitigate challenges, compress the learning curve, and avoid poor decisions.

Mentors are all around us in every organization. Their wisdom comes from their own failures and successes that have generated a depth and breadth of knowledge that is not easily acquired. We should tap them as a resource to serve as part of the think tank in any organization. The cost is minimal, and the advice is priceless.

Epilogue/Conclusion

Listening requires action. Its very definition is to give effort to, pay attention, or give notice of something being said. Listening is broken down into three main types: *effective*, *focused*, and *applied*.

Throughout this book it has been my goal to underscore one simple point—*effective listening* is at the heart of good communications, and it requires attention, understanding, and action. *Focused listening* allows us to develop listening skills that strengthen our understanding. When we consider the context of what is being said and the meaning behind the words, we are putting *applied listening* into action.

Today's emerging leaders need to consistently realize and master the tools of effective listening. This essential concept will ensure that leaders young and experienced alike can work effectively together and provide stronger decision-making. It starts with acknowledging the differences in your organization along with commonalities and how to reconcile them through a shared vision. By applying the listening techniques shared in this book, you are one step closer to mastering this skill. The twenty-first century requires us to be quick, flexible, and adaptive as leaders due to the rapid speed of change. We must embrace this fact with growth and purpose to succeed.

The HURIER model is a model of effective listening that involves hearing, understanding, remembering, interpreting, evaluating, and responding.

A willingness to apply these principles is what allows us to grow as leaders by putting effective listening skills to work in avoiding poor decisions. It represents the needed growth mind-set that empowers us as leaders to exercise the power of applied listening and the importance of meaning in all our communications. This is how we become better leaders in serving our organizations and the people who make them work.

In order to reach our goals as an organization we need to know who we are and where we are going—the ultimate destination. This is where vision is not only essential, it serves as a guide in determining objectives essential to measure our progress in attainment of those goals. Effective listening is what allows us to achieve better understanding of the challenges we face. Without it, we will fail to reach our optimal effectiveness by improving team building, mission planning, and goal setting.

Notes

PREFACE

1. Editorial Team Lutherstadt Wittenberg Marketing GmbH, 1st revised edition 2017. PHOTO CREDITS: Unless otherwise stated, the rights to all photographs reproduced in this brochure are held by Lutherstadt Wittenberg Marketing GmbH (photographers: Johannes Winkelmann, Corinna Kroll, Jan P. Pajak, Jörg P. Pajak). https://www.lutherhochzeit.de/downloads/wittenberg-brochure-en.pdf.

1. FOCUSED LISTENING

1. Michael Laroque, "Top 10 Times Miscommunication Had Awful Consequences," BIZARRE.com, accessed March 1, 2019, https://www.toptenz.net/top-10-times-miscommunication-had-awful-consequences.php.
2. Sims Wyeth, "10 Reasons Eye Contact Is Everything in Public Speaking," *Inc.*, accessed March 1, 2019, https://www.inc.com/sims-wyeth/10-reasons-why-eye-contact-can-change-peoples-perception-of-you.html.
3. Pam Neely, "This Is What Clients Actually Want from Their Ad Agencies | Blog," Whatagraph, accessed February 9, 2019, https://whatagraph.com/blog/articles/this-is-what-clients-actually-want-from-their-ad-agencies.

2. CONSIDERING "MEANING"

1. "Meaning," Merriam-Webster, accessed February 10, 2019, https://www.merriam-webster.com/dictionary/meaning.
2. "Army Military Auxiliary Radio System (MARS)," Facebook, accessed April 11, 2019, https://www.facebook.com/pg/HQArmyMARS/about/?ref=page_internal.
3. "Pony Express Historical Timeline," Pony Express Museum, St. Joseph, MO, accessed March 5, 2019, http://ponyexpress.org/pony-express-historical-timeline/.

4. Kenneth Burke, "How Many Texts Do People Send Every Day (2018)?" Text Request, accessed June 11, 2019, http://www.textrequest.com/blog/how-many-texts-people-send-per-day.

5. Omar Jenblat, "Here's What You Should Know Before Using WhatsApp Business," *Forbes*, June 7, 2018, accessed May 11, 2019, https://www.forbes.com/sites/forbes agencycouncil/2018/06/07/heres-what-you-should-know-before-using-whatsapp-business/#44 6ccccc17e5.

6. Ibid.

7. Steve Nicastro, NerdWallet, USA Today, and Associated Press, "20 Awesome Apps for Small-Business Owners," NerdWallet, January 15, 2019, accessed May 12, 2019, https://www. nerdwallet.com/blog/small-business/20-apps-small-business-owners/.

3. CONSIDERING CONTEXT AND AVOIDING AMBIGUITY

1. Yahya Fakude Ntsikayezwe, "The Importance of Understanding Context in Communication," Medium.com, January 16, 2019, accessed May 5, 2019, https://medium.com/.

2. Carol Kinsey Goman, "How Culture Controls Communication," *Forbes*, November 28, 2011, accessed April 12, 2019, https://www.forbes.com/sites/carolkinseygoman/2011/11/28/how-culture-controls-communication/.

3. Alina Vashurina, "How to Overcome Communication Challenges within a Global Company," Forbes.com, July 3, 2017, accessed April 12, 2019, https://www.forbes.com/sites/forbescommunicationscouncil/2017/07/03/how-to-overcome-communication-challenges-with in-a-global-company/.

4. "Table 1. Persons Obtaining Lawful Permanent Resident Status: Fiscal Years 1820 to 2017," Department of Homeland Security, October 2, 2018, accessed April 12, 2019, https://www.dhs.gov/immigration-statistics/yearbook/2017/table1.

5. "U.S. Immigration Trends," Migrationpolicy.org, February 7, 2019, accessed April 12, 2019, https://www.migrationpolicy.org/programs/data-hub/us-immigration-trends.

6. Barbara B. Adams, PsyD, *Women, Minorities, and Other Extraordinary People* (Austin, TX: Greenleaf Book Group Press, 2018).

7. Artist: The Clash; Album: *Combat Rock*; Released: 1982; Songwriter(s): Topper Headon, Mick Jones, Paul Simonon, Joe Strummer; B-side: "Inoculated City" (1982); "Rush" (1991).

8. "Rob Hall," Wikipedia, accessed March 12, 2019, https://en.wikipedia.org/w/index.php?title=Rob_Hall&oldid=883493617.

9. *Everest*. Directed by Baltasar Kormákur. Produced by Baltasar Kormákur, Tim Bevan, Eric Fellner, Nicky Kentish Barnes, Brian Oliver, and Tyler Thompson, and written by William Nicholson and Simon Beaufoy. Performed by Jason Clarke, Josh Brolin, and John Hawkes. Everest the motion picture © 2019 Universal Pictures Home Entertainment, a Division of NBC Universal.

10. Christopher I. Maxwell, *Lead like a Guide: How World-Class Mountain Guides Inspire Us to Be Better Leaders* (Santa Barbara, CA: Praeger, An Imprint of ABC-CLIO, LLC, 2016).

11. "At Work," Workplace Violence, accessed April 12, 2019, https://www.nsc.org/work-safety/safety-topics/workplace-violence.

12. Sean Coughlan, "2018 Worst Year for US School Shootings," BBC.com, December 12, 2018, accessed May 14, 2019, https://www.bbc.com/news/business-46507514.

13. Megan O'Matz, Stephen Hobbs, and Paula McMahon, "Nikolas Cruz Was Regularly in Trouble at School for Years, Disciplinary Records Show," Sun-sentinel.com, February 17, 2018, accessed March 5, 2019, https://www.sun-sentinel.com/local/broward/fl-school-shooting-nikolas-cruz-discipline-file-20180217-story.html.

14. Paula McMahon, Tonya Alanez, and Lisa J. Huriash, "Parkland Shooter Nikolas Cruz during Confession: 'Kill Me,'" Sun-sentinel.com, February 12, 2019, accessed March 5, 2019,

https://www.sun-sentinel.com/local/broward/parkland/florida-school-shooting/fl-florida-school-shooting-nikolas-cruz-confession-20180806-story.html.

15. Kevin Johnson and Ledyard King, "FBI Failed to Pursue January Tip on Nikolas Cruz, Florida School Shooting Suspect," Usatoday.com, February 16, 2018, accessed March 5, 2019, https://www.usatoday.com/story/news/politics/2018/02/16/fbi-failed-pursue-january-tip-parkland-school-shooter-suspect/345571002/.

4. READY, SET, LISTEN

1. Alan Piper, "What Causes Someone to Constantly Interrupt Others," Quora.com, August 14, 2014, accessed May 11, 2019, https://www.quora.com/What-causes-someone-to-constantly-interrupt-others-when-they-are-talking.

2. Tonja Jacobi and Dylan Schweers, "Female Supreme Court Justices Are Interrupted More by Male Justices and Advocates," *Harvard Business Review*, Hbr.org, April 11, 2017, accessed May 17, 2019, https://hbr.org/2017/04/female-supreme-court-justices-are-interrupted-more-by-male-justices-and-advocates.

3. Leslie Shore, "Gal Interrupted, Why Men Interrupt Women And How to Avert This in the Workplace," Forbes.com, January 3, 2017, accessed May 22, 2019, https://www.forbes.com/sites/womensmedia/2017/01/03/gal-interrupted-why-men-interrupt-women-and-how-to-avert-this-in-the-workplace/#1e66311c17c3.

4. Jenny M. Hoobler, Courtney R. Masterson, Stella M. Nkomo, and Eric J. Michel, "The Business Case for Women Leaders: Meta-Analysis, Research Critique, and Path Forward," Sage Journals.com, March 2, 2016, accessed May 22, 2019, https://journals.sagepub.com/doi/abs/10.1177/0149206316628643.

5. Ibid.

6. Ibid.

7. Jeff McCausland, PhD, retired US Army colonel and founder and CEO of Diamond6 Leadership and Strategy, LLC, "Organizational Culture and Change," lecture, 2018, Eagle Institute, City Tavern, Philadelphia, July 11, 2018, https://www.diamondsixleadership.com/.

8. John Draper, EdD, "Turning Negative Heat into Positive Energy," lecture, 2018 Eagle Institute, Science History Institute, Philadelphia, July 11, 2018, NSPRA National Consultant.

5. CREDIBLE CONVERSATIONS THAT MATTER

1. Eric L. Harvey and Steve Ventura, *Walk the Talk* (Flower Mound, TX: Walk the Talk, 2007).

2. "Enron Scandal," Wikipedia, May 26, 2019, accessed June 12, 2019, https://en.wikipedia.org/wiki/Enron_scandal.

3. Donald T. Phillips, *Lincoln on Leadership: Executive Strategies for Tough Times* (New York: Grand Central, 1992).

4. Doris Kearns Goodwin, *Team of Rivals: The Political Genius of Abraham Lincoln* (London: Penguin Books, 2013).

5. "American Business Awards—International Awards List," Awards List International, accessed May 12, 2019, https://awards-list.com/international-business-awards/american-business-awards/.

6. Syed Balkhi, "Want to Hire 'A' Players? 7 Qualities to Look for in Job Candidates," Business.com, October 9, 2018, accessed June 12, 2019, https://www.business.com/articles/7-qualities-of-top-performers/.

7. "What Makes a Good Accountant?" Foundation Education, February 9, 2017, accessed June 12, 2019, https://www.foundationeducation.edu.au/articles/2016/10/what-makes-a-good-accountant.

6. CONSIDERING LANGUAGE STRUCTURE

1. Joseph Palau, "Giuseppe Verdi: Uniting Italy with Music," *National Geographic History*, January/February 2017.

2. Ibid., https://www.nationalgeographic.com/archaeology-and-history/magazine/2017/01-02/verdi-operas-italy-national-identity/.

3. Thomas Paine, *Common Sense: The Call to Independence*, 1975 ed. (Woodbury, NY: Barron's Educational Series, 1737–1809).

4. *The Citizen's Guide to the Open Public Records Act (OPRA)*. Trenton, NJ: Government Records Council.

5. Simon Sinek, *Start with Why: How Great Leaders Inspire Everyone to Take Action* (New York: Portfolio/Penguin, 2009).

6. Ibid., The golden circle, 137.

7. Rick Warren, *The Purpose-Driven Life: What on Earth Am I Here For?* (Grand Rapids, MI: Zondervan, 2002).

7. WORD CHOICE AND USE

1. Michael Schrage, "Is It OK to Yell at Your Employees?" *Harvard Business Review*, August 7, 2014, accessed May 12, 2019, https://hbr.org/2013/11/is-it-ok-to-yell-at-your-employees.

2. "Theory X and Theory Y: Understanding People's Motivations," Team Management Training from MindTools.com, accessed March 12, 2019, https://www.mindtools.com/pages/article/newLDR_74.htm.

3. Ibid.

4. James C. Collins, *Good to Great: Why Some Companies Make the Leap—and Others Don't* (London: Random House Business, 2001).

5. Matthew Stewart, "Theory U and Theory T, Thoughts on the 50th Anniversary of One of the Most Influential Contributions to Management Theory," *Strategy Business*, August 24, 2010, accessed May 17, 2019, https://www.strategy-business.com/article/00029.

6. Stephen M. R. Covey and R. R. Merrill, *The Speed of Trust: The One Thing That Changes Everything* (New York: Free Press, 2006).

7. Collins, *Good to Great*.

8. B. Male, "The 15 Biggest PR Disasters of the Decade," BusinessInsider.com, 2009, accessed March 12, 2019, https://www.businessinsider.com/.

9. Ibid.

10. Ibid.

11. Ibid.

8. THINKING TOGETHER

1. "The 50 Most Influential Think Tanks in the United States," TheBestSchools.org, October 15, 2015, accessed May 24, 2019, https://thebestschools.org/features/most-influential-think-tanks/.

2. Ibid.

3. "Brain Trust," Merriam-Webster, accessed March 26, 2019, https://www.merriam-webster.com/dictionary/brain%20trust.

4. "ARMY.MIL Features," Army Values, accessed April 2, 2019, https://www.army.mil/values/.

5. Dr. Jack Zenger and Dr. Joseph Folkman, "Why Is It So Difficult for Leaders to Give Positive Feedback?" Zenger Folkman, November 27, 2017, accessed June 12, 2019, https://zengerfolkman.com/articles/why-is-it-so-difficult-for-leaders-to-give-positive-feedback/.

6. Dr. Joseph Folkman, "Why Is It So Difficult for Leaders to Give Positive Feedback?" *Forbes*, October 20, 2017, accessed April 12, 2019, https://www.forbes.com/sites/joefolkman/2017/10/20/why-is-it-so-difficult-for-leaders-to-give-positive-feedback/.

7. Ibid.

8. Stephen C. Betts and Louis J. Pepe, "The Perceived Value of Mentoring: Empirical Development of a Five-Factor Framework," *Journal of Organizational Culture, Communications and Conflict* 10, no. 2 (December 2006): 105–15, accessed May 27, 2019, doi:ISSN 1544-0508.

References

Adams, Barbara B., PsyD. *Women, Minorities, and Other Extraordinary People*. Austin, TX: Greenleaf Book Group Press, 2018.

Balkhi, Syed. "Want to Hire 'A' Players? 7 Qualities to Look for in Job Candidates." Business.com. October 9, 2018. Accessed June 12, 2019. https://www.business.com/articles/7-qualities-of-top-performers/.

Betts, Stephen C., and Louis J. Pepe. "The Perceived Value of Mentoring: Empirical Development of a Five-Factor Framework." *Journal of Organizational Culture, Communications and Conflict* 10, no. 2 (December 2006): 105–15. Accessed May 27, 2019. doi: ISSN 1544-0508.

Brownwell, Judi. "HURIER Model." In *Listening: Attitudes, Principles, and Skills*, 4th ed. New York: Routledge, 2016.

Burke, Kenneth. "How Many Texts Do People Send Every Day (2018)?" Text Request. Accessed June 11, 2019. http://www.textrequest.com/blog/how-many-texts-people-send-per-day.

Collins, James C. *Good to Great: Why Some Companies Make the Leap—and Others Don't.* London: Random House Business, 2001.

Coughlan, Sean. "2018 Worst Year for US School Shootings." BBC.com. December 12, 2018. Accessed May 14, 2019. https://www.bbc.com/news/business-46507514.

Covey, Stephen M. R., and R. R. Merrill. *The Speed of Trust: The One Thing That Changes Everything*. New York: Free Press, 2006.

Folkman, Joseph, Dr. "Why Is It So Difficult for Leaders to Give Positive Feedback?" *Forbes*. October 20, 2017. Accessed April 12, 2019. https://www.forbes.com/sites/joefolkman/2017/10/20/why-is-it-so-difficult-for-leaders-to-give-positive-feedback/.

Goman, Carol Kinsey. "How Culture Controls Communication." *Forbes*. November 28, 2011. Accessed April 12, 2019. https://www.forbes.com/sites/carolkinseygoman/2011/11/28/how-culture-controls-communication/.

Goodwin, Doris Kearns. *Team of Rivals: The Political Genius of Abraham Lincoln*. London: Penguin Books, 2013.

Harvey, Eric L., and Steve Ventura. *Walk the Talk*. Flower Mound, TX: Walk the Talk, 2007.

Hilton, Katherine. "Why Do People Interrupt? It Depends on Whom You're Talking To." TheGuardian.com. May 18, 2018. accessed May 17, 2019. https://www.theguardian.com/lifeandstyle/2018/may/18/why-do-people-interrupt-it-depends-on-whom-youre-talking-to.

Hoobler, Jenny M., Courtney R. Masterson, Stella M. Nkomo, and Eric J. Michel. "The Business Case for Women Leaders: Meta-Analysis, Research Critique, and Path Forward." Sage Journals.com. March 2, 2016. Accessed May 22, 2019. https://journals.sagepub.com/doi/abs/10.1177/0149206316628643.

Jacobi, Tonja, and Dylan Schweers. "Female Supreme Court Justices Are Interrupted More by Male Justices and Advocates." *Harvard Business Review*, Hbr.org. April 11, 2017. Accessed May 17, 2019. https://hbr.org/2017/04/female-supreme-court-justices-are-interrupted-more-by-male-justices-and-advocates.

Jenblat, Omar. "Here's What You Should Know Before Using WhatsApp Business." *Forbes*. June 7, 2018. Accessed May 11, 2019. https://www.forbes.com/sites/forbesagencycouncil/2018/06/07/heres-what-you-should-know-before-using-whatsapp-business/#446ccccc17e5.

Johnson, Kevin, and Ledyard King. "FBI Failed to Pursue January Tip on Nikolas Cruz, Florida School Shooting Suspect." Usatoday.com. February 16, 2018. Accessed March 5, 2019. https://www.usatoday.com/story/news/politics/2018/02/16/fbi-failed-pursue-january-tip-parkland-school-shooter-suspect/345571002/.

Laroque, Michael. "Top 10 Times Miscommunication Had Awful Consequences." BIZARRE.com. Accessed March 1, 2019. https://www.toptenz.net/top-10-times-miscommunication-had-awful-consequences.php.

Lopez, German. "2018 Was by Far the Worst Year on Record for Gun Violence in Schools." Vox.com. December 10, 2018. Accessed March 5, 2019. https://www.vox.com/2018/12/10/18134232/gun-violence-schools-mass-shootings.

Male, B. "The 15 Biggest PR Disasters of the Decade." BusinessInsider.com. 2009. Accessed March 12, 2019. https://www.businessinsider.com/.

Maxwell, Christopher I. *Lead like a Guide: How World-Class Mountain Guides Inspire Us to Be Better Leaders*. Santa Barbara, CA: Praeger, An Imprint of ABC-CLIO, LLC, 2016.

McMahon, Paula, Tonya Alanez, and Lisa J. Huriash. "Parkland Shooter Nikolas Cruz during Confession: 'Kill Me.'" Sun-sentinel.com. February 12, 2019. Accessed March 5, 2019. https://www.sun-sentinel.com/local/broward/parkland/florida-school-shooting/fl-florida-school-shooting-nikolas-cruz-confession-20180806-story.html.

Neely, Pam. "This Is What Clients Actually Want from Their Ad Agencies | Blog." Whatagraph. Accessed February 9, 2019. https://whatagraph.com/blog/articles/this-is-what-clients-actually-want-from-their-ad-agencies.

Nicastro, Steve, NerdWallet, USA Today, and Associated Press. "20 Awesome Apps for Small-Business Owners." NerdWallet. January 15, 2019. Accessed May 12, 2019. https://www.nerdwallet.com/blog/small-business/20-apps-small-business-owners/.

Ntsikayezwe, Yahya Fakude. "The Importance of Understanding Context in Communication." Medium.com. January 16, 2019. Accessed May 5, 2019. https://medium.com/.

O'Matz, Megan, Stephen Hobbs, and Paula McMahon. "Nikolas Cruz Was Regularly in Trouble at School for Years, Disciplinary Records Show." Sun-sentinel.com. February 17, 2018. Accessed March 5, 2019. https://www.sun-sentinel.com/local/broward/fl-school-shooting-nikolas-cruz-discipline-file-20180217-story.html.

Paine, Thomas. *Common Sense: The Call to Independence*. 1975 ed. Woodbury, NY: Barron's Educational Series, 1737–1809.

Palau, Joseph. "Giuseppe Verdi: Uniting Italy with Music." *National Geographic History*. January/February 2017.

Phillips, Donald T. *Lincoln on Leadership: Executive Strategies for Tough Times*. New York: Grand Central, 1992.

Piper, Alan. "What Causes Someone to Constantly Interrupt Others." Quora.com. August 14, 2014. Accessed May 11, 2019. https://www.quora.com/What-causes-someone-to-constantly-interrupt-others-when-they-are-talking.

Schrage, Michael. "Is It OK to Yell at Your Employees?" *Harvard Business Review*. August 7, 2014. Accessed May 12, 2019. https://hbr.org/2013/11/is-it-ok-to-yell-at-your-employees.

Shore, Leslie. "Gal Interrupted, Why Men Interrupt Women and How to Avert This in the Workplace." Forbes.com. January 3, 2017. Accessed May 22, 2019. https://www.forbes.com/sites/womensmedia/2017/01/03/gal-interrupted-why-men-interrupt-women-and-how-to-avert-this-in-the-workplace/#1e66311c17c3.

Sinek, Simon. *Start with Why: How Great Leaders Inspire Everyone to Take Action*. New York: Portfolio/Penguin, 2009.

Stewart, Matthew. "Theory U and Theory T, Thoughts on the 50th Anniversary of One of the Most Influential Contributions to Management Theory." *Strategy Business*. August 24, 2010. Accessed May 17, 2019. https://www.strategy-business.com/article/00029.

The Citizen's Guide to the Open Public Records Act (OPRA). Trenton, NJ: Government Records Council.

Up to the Light. "Client Surveys an Introduction." Brighton, UK: Up to the Light, 2013. http://www.uptothelight.co.uk/.

Vashurina, Alina. "How to Overcome Communication Challenges within a Global Company." Forbes.com. July 3, 2017. Accessed April 12, 2019. https://www.forbes.com/sites/forbescommunicationscouncil/2017/07/03/how-to-overcome-communication-challenges-within-a-global-company/.

Warren, Richard. *The Purpose-Driven Life: What on Earth Am I Here For?* Grand Rapids, MI: Zondervan, 2002.

Wyeth, Sims. "10 Reasons Eye Contact Is Everything in Public Speaking." *Inc.* Accessed March 1, 2019. https://www.inc.com/sims-wyeth/10-reasons-why-eye-contact-can-change-peoples-perception-of-you.html.

Zenger, Jack, Dr., and Dr. Joseph Folkman. "Why Is It So Difficult for Leaders to Give Positive Feedback?" Zenger Folkman. November 27, 2017. Accessed June 12, 2019. https://zengerfolkman.com/articles/why-is-it-so-difficult-for-leaders-to-give-positive-feedback/.

References

About the Author

Louis J. Pepe is the assistant superintendent/CFO for the City of Summit Public Schools in Union County, New Jersey. He has more than thirty years of leadership experience between military, private, and public service focused on leadership, management, operations, and administration.

Lou is a speaker, mentor, and adjunct professor at Montclair State University. His knowledge and success have positioned him as a go-to resource for other professionals throughout the industry. A member of the Oxford Roundtable, Lou presented on Issues in Financing Public Education in America at Oxford University in Oxford, England, in 2005.

He is the president and owner of Lou Pepe Presentations, LLC, consulting on effective management strategies and leadership training through presentations designed for workshops, seminars, conferences, and business meetings.

As a keynote speaker and presenter, Lou has engaged audiences across the country with his down-to-earth, practical advice and insights into today's challenges in managing people and situations to accomplish organizational goals and objectives.

His blog site, http://businessedissues.blogspot.com/, has gained readership from countries all over the world and was featured as "best of blogs" by the American Association of School Administrators.

HONORS AND AWARDS

- School Business Administrator of the Year—New Jersey Association of School Business Officials 2018
- Distinguished Service Award—New Jersey Association of School Business Officials 2018

- Eagle Award 2015 ASBO—Association of School Business Officials International Leadership Achievement Awards
- Pinnacle of Achievement for Innovative Ideas in the field of School Business 2007 ASBO—Association of School Business Officials International
- Oxford Roundtable—2005—Speaker on Issues in Financing Public Education in America, Oxford University, Oxford, England
- Recipient of the US Army Commendation Medal (ARCOM) oak leaf cluster and Achievement Medal

EDUCATION

Pepe earned his bachelor's degree in international business and business administration from Ramapo College of New Jersey and an MBA in finance from William Paterson University's Christos M. Cotsakos College of Business.

BACKGROUND

Prior to entering the field of education, Pepe was a scanning administrator for the Atlantic and Pacific Tea Company, administrative assistant for SL Industries, and served in the US Army Signal Corps as a tactical signal operator 72E in Darmstadt, Germany; USAISC as MARS Radio operator at Fort Campbell, Kentucky; and as an automated telecommunications specialist 72G shift supervisor with the 66th Military Intelligence Brigade, Munich, Germany. Through these experiences, Pepe developed leadership skills in team building, management, and communications.

He is currently a past president of New Jersey Association of School Business Officials, served as a councilman at large in his home community, and continues to serve as a mentor for the New Jersey Department of Education State Certification Program. Lou is on the faculty at Montclair State University as an adjunct professor in the graduate program in education.

He and his wife live in Lincoln Park, New Jersey, and have two daughters and two grandchildren.